There are few safer guides to the themes of John's epistles on the nature of true faith and the experience of assurance than Joel Beeke. Dr Beeke guides us safely through these often stormy waters with the sure touch of a seasoned navigator. In an age when commentaries are getting bigger and heavier, this one, despite its modest length, rises to the top for usefulness and accessibility, reflecting Calvin's description of the best commentators: *brevitas et simplicitas* (brief and simple). This volume exhibits all of the strengths of a preacher-scholar-writer and is warmly recommended.

--Dr. Derek Thomas

This is a thoroughly satisfying and edifying commentary written in today's language and therefore easily read and understood. Dr Beeke brings out the marrow of John's three epistles. He feeds the mind with sound and solid truth and slso challenges the heart to practice obedience and Christian love. It is heartily and unreservedly recommended.

--Rev. Maurice Roberts

# THE EPISTLES OF

# JOHN

Joel Beeke

EVANGELICAL PRESS

 EVANGELICAL PRESS

**Evangelical Press**
Faverdale North Industrial Estate, Darlington, DL3 0PH England
email: sales@evangelicalpress.org

**Evangelical Press USA**
PO Box 825, Webster, NY 14580 USA
email: usa.sales@evangelicalpress.org

www.evangelicalpress.org

First published 2006

Printed and bound in the U. S. A.

Scripture references are from the King James Version

British Library Cataloguing in Publication Data available

ISBN-13  978 0 85234 633 4                    ISBN  0 85234 633 6

With love for

**Jacqueline Markus**

and

**Joanne Timmer**

dear sisters

whose lives display the Christian love

the Apostle John so richly expounds

# Acknowledgements

I am indebted to a number of excellent resources on the epistles of John, which I have highlighted in the 'Further Reading' section of this book. A special thanks to my dear flock, the Heritage Netherlands Reformed Congregation, Grand Rapids, Michigan, for their readiness to 'receive with meekness the engrafted word' (James 1:21) and for their encouragement along the way.

I thank Phyllis TenElshof, Ray B. Lanning, and Kate Timmer for their able assistance with the manuscript. My children, Calvin, Esther, and Lydia, have been patient as ever while I have undertaken this writing project. And without the support of my faithful Mary, my better three-quarters, in whose heart and tongue is the law of kindness, I never would have begun, much less completed, this book.

I pray that you will come away from this Bible study with a deeper appreciation of John's grand gospel themes: fellowship, truth, righteousness, propitiation, self-examination, experiential religion, overcoming worldliness, abiding in Christ, faith, love, joy, sanctification, adoption, and assurance. May the Holy Spirit use this study to conform us more to the image of Christ and pave the way for us to one day 'see him as he is' (1 John 3:2).

**Joel R. Beeke**
Puritan Reformed Theological Seminary
Heritage Netherlands Reformed Congregation
Grand Rapids, Michigan

November 2005

# Contents

Acknowledgements                                                      9

Introduction                                                         11

1. The Essence of the Gospel (1:1-2)                                 19

2. The Goals (1:3-4)                                                 25

3. Walking in Darkness or in the Light (1:5-7)                       33

4. What We Say about Our Sin (1:8-10)                                41

5. Propitiation for Sin (2:1-2)                                      51

6. Assurance of Faith (2:3-6)                                        57

7. The Test of Love (2:7-11)                                         69

8. The Test of Experience (2:12-14)                                  77

9. The Test of Worldliness (2:15-17)                                 89

10. The Test of Sound Doctrine (2:18-27)                             95

11. Abiding in Christ (2:28-29)                                     103

12. Glorious Adoption (3:1-3)                                       111

13. The Contrast Between Righteousness and Sin (3:4-10)             121

14. Loving One Another (3:11-18)                                    131

15. How Christians Should Respond to Doubt (3:19-24)                141

16. Testing False Prophets (4:1-6)                                  149

17. Why We Must Love One Another (4:7-12)                           157

18. Sources of Assurance (4:13-21)                                  165

19. Basic Truths About Faith (5:1-3)                                173

20. Overcoming Worldliness by Faith (5:4-5)                         181

21. God's Testimony of His Son (5:6-12)                             191

22. How to Grow in Assurance (5:13-21)                              203

23. 'For the Truth's Sake' (2 John)                                 215

24. Reactions to the Truth (3 John)                                 225

Study Questions                                                     235

Further Reading                                                     251

# Introduction

No other epistle or letter in the New Testament begins more abruptly than does the First Epistle of John. It has no formal salutation, no personal words of greeting, and no concluding benediction. It is not addressed to a particular church or individual, and therefore is reckoned as one of the catholic or general epistles. After a brief prologue (1:1-4) the writer goes directly to what is on his heart, 'the message which we have heard of him and declare unto you, that God is light, and in him is no darkness at all' (1:5).

## The Author and Date of Composition

The author of this epistle was John, one of Jesus' twelve disciples, known as 'the disciple whom Jesus loved' (John 13:23, 20:2). John and his older brother James, the sons of Zebedee, were Jews from Galilee, brought up to follow their father's trade as fishermen. They were cousins to Jesus; their mother, Salome, was Mary's sister, a devoted follower of Jesus, and eyewitness to his death on the cross and resurrection from the dead.

James and John were among the first disciples Jesus called. When Jesus ordained them, he surnamed them 'Boanerges', or 'the sons of thunder', reflecting the intensity or volatility of their personalities. James and John, with Simon Peter, formed Christ's inner circle among the twelve disciples, and remained with Christ to the end. Both were numbered among the apostles of the infant church. James was the first of the apostles to die, being put to death by Herod around the year 44 (Acts 12:2).

Because John also wrote the gospel bearing his name, he is sometimes called John the evangelist. As author of the Book of Revelation, he is called John the divine (theologian) or John the revelator. Because of the title used in his other epistles, he is also known as John the presbyter or John the elder. All these titles — disciple, apostle, evangelist, divine, revelator, and presbyter — refer to one and the same John.

As in his gospel, so in his epistles, John seems reticent to mention his own name. His use of terms such as 'beloved' and 'my little children' indicate that he was so well known to his readers that he did not need to mention his name. He does make it clear that he was an apostle and eyewitness to 'that which was from the beginning' (1:1), distinguishing sharply between 'we' (apostles), 'you' (readers), and 'they' (false teachers) (see 1:1-3; 4:14).

The style, vocabulary, and emphases of this epistle and the gospel of John are so similar that most scholars agree that one man was the author of both works. Both use simple vocabulary to communicate profound truths. Both frequently deal in contrasts; here in his first epistle, John distinguishes between light and darkness (1:5), loving God and loving the world (2:15-17), truth and falsehood (2:20-21), eternal life and eternal death (3:14).

The ancient church universally attributed this epistle to John. Polycarp, a Christian leader in Asia Minor who died as a martyr around 155 A.D., was a disciple of John and cited this epistle as John's writing. So did Irenaeus, disciple of Polycarp, reckoned as the first great theologian of the church. In fact, all the Greek and Latin church fathers assumed this epistle was written by John.

Early Christian writers tell us that in later years John lived in Ephesus, a city of Lydia on the coast of Asia Minor. He laboured among the churches there and in other nearby places where Paul had planted churches on his missionary journeys. The 'seven churches which are in Asia' (Rev. 1:11), to which the Book of Revelation was first sent, were part of this field of labour.

Held to be the youngest of the apostles, John survived all the others and lived to a great old age, dying peacefully, according to Polycarp, at Ephesus during the reign of the Roman emperor Trajan, 98-117 A.D. His first epistle was probably written between 85 and 95 A.D., after the gospel of John and before persecution broke out during the reign of Domitian (81-96 A.D.).

## The Background: False Teachings, Corrupt Practices

Generally speaking, the New Testament epistles were written in response to certain situations and problems that came to the attention of the apostles. Some were written to offer comfort to Christians under various trials, facing hardships, or enduring persecution. Some were written to confront wrongdoing in the church and to call erring church members to repentance.

Others were written because false teachers had appeared in the church and threatened to lead Christians away from the foundation of true faith and practice laid down by Christ and his apostles. These epistles served to remind Christians of those foundational truths and practices, and to help them recognize the heretical teachings and corrupt ways of the false teachers. Such was John's first epistle. John does not mince words: 'Who is a liar but he that denieth that Jesus is the Christ? He is antichrist, that denieth the Father and the Son' (2:22). Two chapters later John warns against naively embracing false teachers and their doctrines: 'Beloved, believe not every spirit, but try the spirits whether they are of God: because many false prophets are gone out in the world' (4:1).

Central to the true gospel is the claim that God, in the person of his eternal Son, 'was made flesh, and dwelt among us' (John 1:14), incarnated as the Lord Jesus Christ. 'God was manifest in the flesh' was the first article of faith among Christians (1 Tim. 3:16). This foundational truth of the incarnation was a stumbling block to many Gentiles and to many Jews who had been influenced by the prevailing Gentile or Greek religious and philosophical thought of the day.

At least as far back as Plato, Greek thinkers had embraced a dualistic view of the nature of things, which held that the difference between spirit and flesh is nothing less than the difference between good and evil. God, being a Spirit, is wholly good; man, being a spirit dwelling in a body of flesh, must therefore be a mixture of good and evil. Thus it would be impossible that God, being wholly good, could or would join himself to an evil body of flesh and blood, and so mingle the precious with the vile. Those who took this view were compelled to reject the incarnation outright, or else find a way to explain it away. Thus, they were compelled to deny 'that Jesus Christ is come in the flesh' (4:2).

Two heresies developed among those who tried to understand and interpret Christianity in terms of Greek thought. The first was Gnosticism, from *gnosis,* the Greek word for knowledge. There were nearly as many versions of Gnosticism as there were Gnostic teachers. Central to all forms of Gnosticism was the idea that salvation is being delivered from the body and its dominion. This deliverance was achieved by attaining enlightenment and the knowledge of mysteries, imparted by special divine revelation. What mattered about the gospel, or Scripture in general, was not its literal meaning but the hidden spiritual meanings these Gnostics claimed had been made known only to them.

The second heresy was Docetism, from *dokeo,* a Greek verb meaning 'to seem' or 'to appear'. Like the Gnostics they denied the full humanity of Christ. They held that Christ only 'seemed' or 'appeared' to be human. They distinguished between Christ and Jesus, holding that the divine Christ had descended upon the human Jesus at the time of his baptism and departed from him at the cross. There was therefore no real union of the human and the divine natures, but only the fleeting appearance of a union.

Both these heresies affected the way believers in John's day lived, but in surprisingly different ways. Some held that because the body is evil, it must be subdued with harsh rigour and be denied every kind of satisfaction or pleasure. Paul describes the early beginnings of this Gnostic asceticism in Colossians 2:16-23.

Others turned to hedonism, the unbridled pursuit of pleasure. Gnosticism enabled them to draw a sharp line between their spiritual lives and 'the things done in the body'. The sins of the flesh, forbidden to ordinary men, became matters of indifference to those who had been enlightened. Sin was no longer sin, so why not indulge? In the second and third centuries this view led Gnostic churches to practise the grossest forms of immorality, even in public worship.

One of the leading Gnostic teachers at Ephesus in John's day was Cerinthus, a Jew from Alexandria and disciple of the Jewish Platonist philosopher, Philo. John knew Cerinthus and regarded him as an enemy. Irenaeus relates a story told by Polycarp of a time John entered the public baths at Ephesus. When he discovered that Cerinthus was there, John rushed out without bathing, exclaiming, 'Let us leave at once, let the bath-house be destroyed, for Cerinthus, the enemy of the truth, is within.'

In his first epistle, John does not rebuke Cerinthus or indulge in a point-by-point refutation of his teaching. He doesn't even mention Cerinthus by name. Rather, John deals with the problems of Gnosticism and Docetism by reasserting the gospel that he and the other apostles proclaimed, focusing on those points that refute the heresies that were creeping into the churches. John affirms that God came to earth, joining his glory to our frailty in the person of his Son to save sinners.

Having reasserted this truth, John goes on to explain the doctrinal, experiential, and ethical implications of that gospel, so that those in the church could examine themselves and know whether or not what they believed and practised was the real gospel. He makes clear that sin ruptures our relationship with God and sentences us to everlasting ruin if grace doesn't intervene. True believers would be encouraged and strengthened by this teaching, while those who were tainted with Gnosticism, Docetism, or other heresies would be exposed and ashamed.

Notice the wisdom of John's approach. Rather than a narrowly focused treatment applying only to believers in Asia

Minor in the first century, his epistle becomes relevant for every generation of Christians. Every Christian has to contend with deviations from the truth as well as with moral corruptions fostered by Satan. John presents the gospel and its implications for daily living in such a way that Christians in any age will find truth, light, and guidance for daily living.

Remember John's point that poisonous teaching and 'false prophets', as he calls them in chapter 4, verse 1, originated within the church. 'They went out from us, but they were not of us; for if they had been of us, they would no doubt have continued with us' (2:19). From its beginning, the Christian church has had problems of this kind. There never was a time when the church was free of heresy, internal turmoil, and persecution. Today, as in John's day, the church's greatest danger comes from within the church, not from without. The great persecutions that have assaulted the church from without have only strengthened the church.

## The Journey to Fulness of Joy

With this background in mind, we will now set out to discover the many lessons John has to teach us in his First Epistle. We should keep in mind that John's purpose from first to last is positive, not negative. He begins by saying, 'These things write we unto you, that your joy may be full' (1:4). He ends by declaring, 'These things have I written unto you that believe on the name of the Son of God; that ye may know that ye have eternal life, and ye may believe on the name of the Son of God' (5:13). The goal is fulness of joy for every Christian. The starting point is true faith in Christ. The road to joy lies in the way of abiding in Christ, increasing knowledge, deepening faith, perfecting obedience, and attaining full assurance. Let us start this journey together, calling upon the Triune God for help and direction in the study, interpretation, and application of this portion of the God-breathed Holy Scriptures:

> Blessed Lord, who hast caused all holy Scriptures to be written for our learning: Grant that we may in such wise

hear them, read, mark, learn, and inwardly digest them, that by patience and comfort of thy holy Word, we may embrace and ever hold fast the blessed hope of everlasting life, which thou hast given us in our Saviour Jesus Christ. Amen.

*Book of Common Prayer,* 1662

# 1

# *The Essence of the Gospel*

*That which was from the beginning, which we have heard, which we have seen with our eyes, which we have looked upon, and our hands have handled, of the Word of life; (for the life was manifested, and we have seen it, and bear witness, and show unto you that eternal life, which was with the Father, and was manifested unto us;) (1 John 1:1–2).*

In his celebrated gospel, the Apostle John presented Jesus Christ evangelistically (20:31). Now, in 1 John, he explains pastorally what it means to be in Christ and how to find assurance of faith and fulness of joy (1:4).

The opening verses take us from eternity past to eternity future, summarizing the gospel's teaching about the Lord Jesus. He is the good news of the gospel; he is the essence of the message proclaimed by the apostles. John says four important things about him.

## The Eternal Son of God

Jesus is 'that which was from the beginning'. John is not thinking here about the birth of Jesus or the beginning of his earthly ministry. He uses this expression to signify that Jesus existed before anything else. His words echo Genesis 1:1. When everything else began to have existence, Jesus the Word of life was already present. He did not have to come into being. He already was. He is the unmade, uncreated one. He is and was and ever will be the complete and perfect Word of life.

Jesus himself spoke of his eternal being. 'Before Abraham was, I am', he told his disciples (John 8:58). He also spoke of his eternal pre-existence when he prayed, 'O Father, glorify thou me with thine own self with the glory which I had with thee before the world was' (John 17:5).

John's words also echo the first words of his gospel: 'In the beginning was the Word, and the Word was with God, and the Word was God' (John 1:1; cf. Prov. 8:22–23). The Word of whom he speaks is Jesus Christ, the eternal Son of God, the second person of the Trinity, the everlasting Lord, the eternal I AM who is and was and is to come, the One who has given life to everything else.

What comfort, what strength, what security we receive from knowing that our Saviour is the eternal Son of God! Everything else perishes and grows old like worn-out clothing, but Christ remains; his years have no end (Heb. 1:10-12).

## The Incarnate Saviour

The eternal experienced the temporal. He became 'that which … we have heard, which we have seen with our eyes, which we have looked upon, and our hands have handled, of the Word of life' (1:1). He became a real man. He who was ever with the Father became flesh and lived among us (John 1:14).

John speaks in the first person plural 'we', referring to himself and his fellow apostles, whose eyewitness accounts are authoritative for the church. John says, 'we' heard Jesus speak, 'we' saw what he did, 'we' observed how he lived, and 'we' touched him with our hands. John and the other disciples had lived and traveled with Jesus for three years. They had beheld his glory!

John first heard about Jesus from John the Baptist (John 1:29). He heard gracious words from Jesus' lips, calling John to follow him. He heard Jesus speak of the work he had come to earth to do. He heard Jesus cry in the midst of suffering, 'Father, forgive them; for they know not what they do' (Luke 23:34). He watched as Jesus uttered in agony from the cross, 'My God, my God, why hast thou forsaken me?' (Matt. 27:46).

John also saw Jesus with his own eyes. He saw the Word made flesh in Jesus' ministry, in his transfiguration, in Gethsemane, and on the cross. John saw the blood trickle from Jesus' head, hands, back, and feet; he saw Immanuel in agony. And he saw Christ's glory manifested in his miracles.

But John saw Jesus with eyes of understanding, as 'the only begotten of the Father, full of grace and truth' (John 1:14). He looked upon Jesus as the divine Teacher, the Physician of souls, the Defender of the weak, the Light of the world, the Servant of servants at the last supper, the great Sufferer and Intercessor, the uplifted Saviour, the Conqueror of death, and the ascended King.

John also touched the Saviour. He placed his arm on Christ's arm and leaned his head upon Jesus' bosom. Jesus, who was in the bosom of his Father, manifested himself to John and the apostles, so that they could have a place in the bosom of the eternal Christ.

John knew from personal experience that Jesus was no phantom, no ghost, no mere spirit. He was a real man of flesh and blood. If you pricked Jesus with a needle, he would bleed. If you injured him, he would wince like any other man.

## The God-Man

John thus affirms both the humanity and divinity of Jesus as necessary for him to be a true Saviour and Mediator. To bear the heavy burden of God's infinite wrath against him, Jesus must himself be God. Yet to be man's substitute before God, Jesus must truly be man. Salvation is in no other (Acts 4:12); 'there is one God, and one mediator between God and men, the man Christ Jesus' (1 Tim. 2:5). Do we believe these truths about Jesus with all our mind and soul? When Jesus is presented to us, what do we do with him? What do we hear from him? What do we see in him? How do we handle the Word of Life?

John's passion was proclaiming Jesus Christ as God-man Saviour. His great joy was to share with others all that he had heard with his ears, seen with his eyes, and handled with his hands — the eternal Word of Life. Christ was the Alpha and Omega of John's ministry.

## The Communicator of Life

Finally, John tells us that Jesus, who is from the beginning and of whom we have seen and heard, is 'the Word of life'. 'The life was manifested, and we have seen it, and bear witness, and show unto you that eternal life, which was with the Father, and was manifested unto us' (1:2).

We use words to express our thoughts. Christ's words express the thoughts of the Father, because God speaks by the mouth of his Son. John calls Jesus Christ the Word: 'In the beginning was the Word, and the Word was with God, and the Word was God' (1:1). As eternal God, Jesus Christ communicated physical and material life to the world. He was there when God said, 'Let there be light: and there was light' (Gen. 1:3). He was there when God said, 'Let us make man in our image, after our likeness' (Gen. 1:26). He was there when God breathed into man the breath of life, and man became a living soul. As eternal God, he created and sustains all things in this world. In becoming man, he communicated to this world the kind of life that man should live before God, in perfect conformity with God's law.

But John also tells us that Jesus is the Word of true, heavenly life that transcends the material world. He is the Eternal Life that was with the Father, and he has come into this world to communicate eternal life to those who cannot have fellowship with a holy God because of sin.

John heard Jesus say, 'As the Father raiseth up the dead, and quickeneth them; even so the Son quickeneth whom he will' (John 5:21). He heard Jesus, the Good Shepherd, say, 'My sheep hear my voice, and I know them, and they follow me:

and I give unto them eternal life' (John 10:27–28). Truly, Jesus Christ came to bring life.

## Conclusion

John presents the essence of the gospel in these two opening verses (1:1-2). Reaffirming the foundational truths of the Christian faith about the person and work of the Lord Jesus Christ, he answers the false teaching that was becoming prevalent in the first century.

This Saviour also answers the needs of our hearts today. Everyone of us by nature is in a state of death and enmity against God. Because of our sin we cannot be accepted by God. We cannot come to God by our own efforts or through our own merits. We are as much the enemies of God as those who long ago denied the humanity of Jesus. If we have not embraced the gospel of Jesus Christ by faith, we are clinging to some kind of heresy in our lives, too. We have not come to believe *the truth* that God has made known about his Son.

God comes to the aid of sinners through Christ, the Word of life, who has come into this world to reconcile them with himself through the blood of his cross. Life — eternal life — is manifested to us from the Father by the Son.

# 2

# *The Goals*

*That which we have seen and heard declare we unto you, that ye also may have fellowship with us: and truly our fellowship is with the Father, and with his Son Jesus Christ. And these things write we unto you, that your joy may be full* (1 John 1:3–4).

John has four practical goals in view in writing his first epistle. He wants to promote fellowship with Christ's apostles and the saints, fellowship with God, fulness of joy, and assurance of faith. The first three of these goals come to the surface already in these verses.

John could argue directly against heresy, but he did not choose that approach. Instead, he shows us how to know and experience true Christian fellowship, joy, and assurance.

## Fellowship with One Another

John ties together true fellowship among believers and the truths of the gospel preached by the apostles with true fellowship with God in Christ: 'That which we have seen and heard declare we unto you, that ye also may have fellowship with us: and truly our fellowship is with the Father, and with his Son Jesus Christ' (1:3). John's focus on 'we' — *we* have seen and *we* have heard — refers, first of all, to the apostles of the New Testament. John

is making apostolicity a necessary attribute of the church. As the
Nicene Creed affirms, Christians believe in 'one, holy, catholic,
and apostolic church'.

The church and its fellowship are built on the foundation
of the apostles and prophets. Christ himself is the cornerstone
(Eph. 2:20). Apostles were eyewitnesses of Jesus' ministry,
death, and resurrection (Acts 1:22). They, along with the prophets, were spokesmen for the Saviour (John 14:26, 15:26). They
wrote the Scriptures, which the church recognized as canonical
for faith and practice. The written Word of God is thus the norm
by which the life of the church is to be measured. The church
can be one, holy, and catholic only insofar as she is an apostolic
church founded upon Christ alone.

John asserts that confession of the apostolic faith is a *sine
qua non* of true Christian fellowship: 'that ye also may have
fellowship with us' (1:3). Based on biblical, apostolic doctrine,
Christians have fellowship with the apostles and with one another. John writes to promote such fellowship among believers
who, based on the apostolic faith, trust Christ alone for salvation.

Authentic Christian fellowship is based on the apostolic
truths of knowing who Jesus is, what the gospel is, and what
Christ has done for us. Such fellowship begins with a believ-
er's reconciliation with the Father through Christ. As John says,
'Truly our fellowship is with the Father, and with his Son Jesus
Christ' (1:3).

God's spiritual children grow in the knowledge of apostolic
truth and the joy of true fellowship. This fellowship is not the
superficial attachment of random individuals, but the profound
mutual relationship of those who abide in Christ and in truth,
and therefore belong to one other. This fellowship expands by
searching the apostles' doctrine together, speaking from heart to
heart about the ways of God, and being helping hands to one
another. When fellow believers grow, we grow; when they rejoice, we rejoice; when they weep, we weep. When they fall into
sin, we care enough to lovingly confront them, restoring them
to fellowship with God and his people. True believers ought to
comfort each other in love (Prov. 17:17), encourage and edify

each other (Ps. 55:14; Rom. 14:19), talk and share with each another (Mal. 3:16), admonish each other in love (Ps. 141:5), and pray with each other (Acts 1:14).

Are you increasingly experiencing that kind of fellowship? Do you strive to grow in a deeper, more profound experience of apostolic truth and in communion with the Lord's people? If we truly know Jesus Christ and have experienced his salvation, then we will increasingly want to grow in the apostles' doctrine and to unite with others who also share that joy.

## Fellowship with God

Fellowship or communion with God is a glorious privilege. It is made possible only through faith in Jesus Christ, who was sent not only to redeem sinners but to restore them to fellowship with God. The great goal of the gospel is that we might know communion with the living and true God.

The Greek word *koinonia* was occasionally used in Greek culture to describe the marriage relationship. How appropriate then that believers should be spoken of as those who have *koinonia* — intimate fellowship — with Christ! Children of God have been married to Christ in the gospel. The foundation of that communion is not in us but in God. Thoughts of communing with the saints were the joy of Christ's heart from eternity. We therefore must look not to ourselves but to Christ, for the gospel comes from God to us and never from us to him. He only seeks our response to that love, which quickens and ignites us.

This God-centred focus is desperately needed today. As we lament our own sinfulness, we ought to do so in the light of Christ's glorious coming to us in grace.

The communion that believers enjoy with God is grounded in and sustained by the apostolic gospel. People are deceived who claim to have fellowship with God while walking in darkness and while disbelieving the Spirit-inspired eyewitness testimony of the apostles (1:6).

Thus there can be no disharmony between devotion and doctrine, for true devotion is grounded in God's self-revelation, his Word. The Christ we have communion with is the revealed Christ of Holy Scripture, not an imagined or reconstructed Christ. Communion with God is reserved only for those who have been brought by God's grace to know and confess the apostolic gospel and who have experienced its saving grace and power in their lives.

There is no other way of entering into communion with God than through this gospel. Those who are in true communion with God have been captivated by the revealed gospel of his Son, Jesus Christ.

When we commune with God, the spotlight of that communion often focuses on one Person of the Trinity. The believer has fellowship with individual Persons of the Godhead. We have fellowship with the Father in *love*. The Father delights to bestow divine love on every believer. 'The Father himself loveth you', Jesus said (John 16:27).

The way to exercise communion with the Father is to receive and return his love by faith through Christ. As the believer rests in the bosom of the Father through Christ, he returns the love in his heart to the heart of the Father, from whom it originated. We love the Father by trusting in his Son, by delighting in the Father himself, by reverencing his Word and his work in his people, and by obeying his law.

When a Christian encounters obstacles in loving God, he must think of the nature of the Father's love. His love comes first and is unchangeable. God has proved that at the cross of Christ. Those who come to the Father with such meditations will find assurance of the Father's love.

The special characteristic of fellowship with Christ is *grace,* received by faith. 'Of his fulness have all we received, and grace for grace' (John 1:16). Christ is the essence of grace.

There is no end to the gracious privileges believers enjoy in Christ. Through adoption into God's family, believers by grace commune with Christ as their brother. Christ is not ashamed to call believers family, for they have that kind of communion. Believers also commune with Christ as willing servants. They are servants, brothers, and adopted children of the living God through Jesus Christ, who is firstborn among many brothers

and sisters. Through communing with Christ, we know God as
our Father and Christ as our Elder Brother. That helps assure us
that Christ belongs to us and we to him.

John does not directly focus on the Spirit in 1 John 1:3. Perhaps that is because the special ministry of the Spirit is bringing
us the precious promises of the Father and the blessings of the
gospel in his Son. Perhaps the doctrines being denied by the
Gnostics are related to the Fatherhood of God and the Sonship
of Christ. But we must never forget that when we commune
with the Father and the Son, it is always by the Spirit.

We have fellowship with the Holy Spirit as *Comforter*. The
Spirit helps the believer remember the words of Christ and
teaches him what they mean. He glorifies Christ. He spreads the
love of God in the Christian's heart. He convinces the believer
that he is a child of God. He seals faith in the Christian. He assures the believer of faith, anoints him, adopts him, and grants
him the Spirit of supplication.

Communion with the living God is the consummate fruit
of the gospel. It places us, as a Puritan said, 'into the very sub-
urbs of heaven'. Communion with God now prepares us for
that endless face-to-face communion that we will one day enjoy
with God.

Do you know something of this communion with God?
Then you too will exclaim through the Spirit, 'Our fellowship is
with the Father, and with his Son Jesus Christ.'

## Fulness of Joy

Do you know anyone who does not want more joy in life? Fellowship with God is the fountain of joy. It come from knowing
the love of God as our Father in heaven, receiving the grace and
gifts of our Lord Jesus Christ, and experiencing the communion
of the Holy Spirit (2 Cor. 13:14). Fellowship and joy come together when God's people commune with one another through
the Spirit as they worship God the Father and God the Son.

Joy is an emotional response to whatever causes pleasure
or delight, lifts our spirits, and induces a feeling of satisfaction,
well-being, or blessedness. Joy can be found in many things

— in work, in possessions, in personal achievements, in rec-
reations and pastimes, in human relationships. A certain kind
of joy can even be found, temporarily, in 'the pleasures of sin'
(Heb. 11:25). But John has in mind a greater joy than all these,
a joy found only in God, a joy that is unique to the followers of
Jesus Christ.

Many people seem to lead a life of unending misery, finding joy in nothing, one day following another in unrewarding
toil, frustration, disappointment, and heartache.  Others find a
measure of joy in their daily activities and relationships, whether
lawful or sinful, but that joy is elusive, fleeting, and subject to a
painful law of diminishing returns.

Even Christians make the mistake of looking for joy in the
wrong places, or settling for something much less than what
John desires for us, namely, 'that your joy may be full'.

John borrows this phrase from the Lord Jesus Christ. Christ
spoke of himself as 'the true vine', of which believers are branches. For them, life and fruitfulness depend on abiding in him and
in his love, doing the things he commands. Christ then declares,
'These things I have spoken unto you, that my joy might remain
in you, and that your joy might be full' (John 15:11). In the next
chapter, Christ bestows on all Christians the privilege of praying
in his name, and then adds, 'Hitherto have ye asked nothing in
my name: ask, and ye shall receive that your joy may be full'
(John 16:24).

In both instances Christ promises a joy that is greater, more
complete, and more abiding than any other. This joy comes to
a Christian who abides in Christ, experiencing the love of God
in Christ and doing the things that please Christ. This joy is also
found in discovering how willingly God hears prayers offered in
the Name of Christ, and his power to answer such prayers, according to Christ's own promise.

John now takes up this theme and declares this joy to be his
third purpose in writing the things found in his epistle. In knowing and doing these things our joy shall be full, or more literally
translated, 'be made full'.

This statement opens the entire epistle. It is not necessary
here to do more than summarize a few of the many things that

contribute to the fulness of joy experienced by Christians.

- There is the joy of knowing God, and his love in Christ, and knowing that our sins are forgiven and that we have eternal life, summed up by John as 'the message which we have heard of him' (1 John 1:5; 2:1,2; 3:1, 4:16; 5:1). True joy is always ultimately Christ-centred. Truly, we rejoice most when we enjoy Christ most; joy ceases to be joy when it becomes unhinged from Christ.

- There is the joy that comes from doing those things which God commands, the things that please him (3:22). We discover the great joy of the will of God when we obey the revealed will of God. Joy and obedience reinforce each other. This obedience especially entails believing on the name of his Son Jesus Christ and loving one another (3:23), and so having fellowship with God — dwelling in God and God dwelling in us, as our portion in this life (3:24).

- There is the joy produced by the work of the Holy Spirit in our lives as the 'unction from the Holy One', teaching us all things, being the great power by which we overcome the world, the flesh, and the 'wicked one', and bringing us to full assurance of grace and salvation (2:20,27; 3:24; 4:4,13). Such joy, by the Spirit's grace, becomes a disciplined state of mind in mature believers, and results in satisfied and contented living (Phil. 4:11).

- There is the joy of communing with other believers that reinforces joy in God (1 John 3:10-24). If you are a believer, you have experienced that kind of joy. When you were feeling down, you communed with another believer, and the Spirit of Christ restored your joy. Perhaps you did not feel like speaking to

another believer, but you knew from past experience
that you would find more joy if you did so. God
knows how to turn our spurs of sorrow into wings
of joy. He honours his people when they fellowship
with him and with other believers.

In all these ways God gives fruit-bearing joy to his believing children in and through his Son, Jesus Christ. 'The Christian should be an alleluia from head to foot', wrote Augustine.
Luther put it this way: 'The Christian ought to be a living doxol-
ogy.' How inconsistent we are about rejoicing in God through
communing with him!

We must ask ourselves: Do people see in how we live that
communion with God is what gives us true joy? Are the three
purposes that John sets forth in the introduction of his epistle
— fellowship with believers, fellowship with the Father and the
Son, and true joy — also the purposes of our lives? If not, your
lack of joy shows that your Christianity is leaking somewhere.

How can we experience these rivers of unfailing joy? By
doing two things. First, quit seeking your joys in earthly things.
Second, look to Jesus by faith. Since Jesus is the source of all
true joy, this joy holds the promise of reaching as high, as wide,
as deep as God himself, and lasting just as long; a treasure to
be enjoyed in this life and in the life to come. As Robert Murray M'Cheyne says so beautifully, 'Believe not [in Jesus], and
you will have no joy. Believe little, and you will have little joy.
Believe much, and you will have much joy. Believe all, and you
will have all joy, and your joy shall be full.'

# 3

# Walking in Darkness or in the Light

> This then is the message which we have heard of him,
> and declare unto you, that God is light, and in him is no
> darkness at all. If we say that we have fellowship with
> him, and walk in darkness, we lie, and do not the truth:
> but if we walk in the light, as he is in the light, we have
> fellowship one with another, and the blood of Jesus
> Christ his Son cleanseth us from all sin (1 John 1:5–7).

Fellowship with the God of light is evidence of the power of the
gospel in our lives. John introduces that theme here, and sub-
sequently applies it personally so that those who read his letter
can examine where they stand in the light of God's Word. That,
in turn, enables them to confront the errors of those who try to
lead them astray.

## This Message is from God

John stresses throughout his epistle that he preaches God's
Word, not his own. 'This then is the message which we have
heard of him, and declare unto you' (1:5). John is simply repeating and applying what Jesus taught. If anyone despises this
teaching, he despises God.

Those who proclaim this gospel today have the same man-
date. We have no authority to do anything other than to repeat

and apply what God has revealed in his Word. If ministers or evangelists water down the message of the gospel, or add anything to that message to make it more appealing, we no longer are proclaiming the gospel.

John affirms this gospel in verses 5–7, first, by affirming that 'God is light, and in him is no darkness at all', and then by explaining the practical implications of this affirmation. He tells about the dangers of deceiving ourselves by walking in darkness, then about what it means to walk in the light of the cleansing blood of Christ.

**The God of Light**

John affirms in verse 5 that 'God is light'. John begins here because this is where the gospel begins. The gospel does not begin with man and his needs. It begins with God and the character of God. Paul begins his epistle to the Romans by telling us that God is righteous and that the gospel reveals his righteousness. That is precisely what John does in his first epistle. He does not just affirm God's existence; he tells us what God is like.

We know God exists by looking at his work in this world. Our observation tells us certain things about God's being — that he is supremely powerful and intelligent. John offers us more. He describes God's moral character. You cannot deduce that from seeing God's work around about you.

'The heavens declare the glory of God' (Ps. 19:1); they shout that God exists. But the heavens are limited in telling us what God is like. Is he good? Is he merciful? Does he love me? What will he do with me when I die? The heavens remain silent to the deeper longings of our hearts. To understand God's moral character, God must reveal that character to us.

So John tells us, 'God is light'. He learned that from Jesus. Jesus also said, 'I am the light of the world: he that followeth me shall not walk in darkness, but shall have the light of life' (John 8:12).

God dwells in unapproachable light. He is as high above us as the heavens are above the earth, but he has chosen in his mercy to reveal himself to us. He has pulled back the curtain to show us what the heavens can never show us — his very heart and mind. 'This is the message that we have heard from him', says John.

To be saved by God, we need to go to the One in whom God revealed his heart and his mind, Jesus Christ. 'If you have seen me', said Jesus, 'you have seen the Father; I and the Father are one.' This is the gospel that we herald to the world: God himself is revealed in the life and death and resurrection of his Son. This is the revelation of the holy God of heaven.

## A God without Darkness

Because the aim of the gospel is to bring men into fellowship with God, we need to know what God is like. John tells us that 'God is light' and then adds, 'in him is no darkness at all'. In the Greek, John actually uses a kind of double negative. Translated literally, he says, 'And darkness in him—no, none at all!'

Often in Scripture the term *light* signifies purity, life-giving power, glory, wisdom, or knowledge. *Darkness* often signifies ignorance, evil, corruption, and death. It is often connected to Satan as the prince of darkness and to the darkness of men's hearts by nature.

With regard to God, Paul talks about light as knowing the glory of God (2 Cor. 4:6). But there is another, deeper sense in which light is used to reflect what God is in himself. John does not say that God *brings* light, or that God *gives light,* but that 'God *is* light'. God is light, the Holy One, the faithful and true, the One who is glorious in holiness, fearful in praises, whose light shines in the darkness of our hearts and enables us to walk in his light (John 1:5; 1 John 2:8). David confesses in Psalm 36:

> *The fountain of eternal life*
> *Is found alone with thee,*
> *And in the brightness of thy light*
> *We clearly light shall see.*

Psalter 94:4

There is no defect in the character of God. His holiness and purity and righteousness are perfect. Next to this everything else is tarnished and unclean. In God's sight the very heavens are unclean and the holy angels are charged with folly (Job 4:18). No wonder Paul said of God, 'Who only hath immortality, dwelling in the light which no man can approach unto; whom no man hath seen, nor can see: to whom be honour and power everlasting' (1 Tim. 6:16). God is 'the Father of lights, with whom is no variableness, neither shadow of turning' (James 1:17). God is pure, unadulterated light.

In God there are no dark corners, no shadows, no moral inconsistencies. God is eternally and implacably opposed to sin. His eyes are too pure to look upon sin. He sees every wicked way in us. That thought frightens us, for many of us want a God who will let us live as we please; we want a God who is benign, who will never interfere, who will stand on the sidelines. But the God and Father of our Lord Jesus Christ is pure and holy. He will not tolerate wickedness.

## The Kingdoms of Light and Darkness

John contrasts two kingdoms that are absolutely opposed to one another. He says there is a realm of darkness in this world that is controlled by sin, error, and evil. Nothing in this kingdom of darkness is found in God, for God is true, unadulterated light.

When Jesus was about to be crucified, he said, 'Now is the hour that this world has been given; now is the hour of darkness, now the prince of this world, the prince of darkness has come, but he has nothing in me' (cf. Luke 22:53; John 14:30). There was nothing in Jesus that Satan, the prince of darkness, could overrule.

The kingdom of darkness is characterized by sin, falsehood, evil, error, heresy, and corruption. The kingdom of light is characterized by holiness, purity, righteousness, and truth. Between these two kingdoms there is a great gulf that cannot be bridged by man.

To understand the difference between gospel truth and heresy, we must begin by knowing who God is and what he is like. So much of what passes for gospel thinking today does not begin here; rather, it starts with man and his needs. What happens, then, is that people begin to think of God only in terms of convenience — God is someone whose chief responsibility is to make people happy and to make sure that they get through life comfortably. They begin to ask questions like: 'If God is a God of love, why doesn't he meet my needs? Why doesn't God stop wars and famines? Why doesn't God deliver me from my troubles?'

Whenever people talk like that, you can be sure they do not understand that God belongs to a dominion that is outside and above what man has done in his deep fall into darkness and his ongoing sin. If God so desired, he could leave every one of us in that darkness because that is what we deserve. God does not owe anyone in this world anything.

Do we know the holy God of light, or do we make a god of our feelings and our desires? By nature, self is the beginning, centre, and end of our personal universe. I once saw a large poster of the earth, on top of which stood a tiny man who declared, 'I am the god of this universe; the earth revolves around me.' If we are like that man in whom self reigns, we proclaim that we live and move in the realm of darkness. When we truly come to know that God is light, our focus shifts from ourselves to him.

John answers the question of how we can have fellowship with the God of holy light from both a negative and a positive perspective in verses 6 and 7 by using an old biblical metaphor of 'walking' for one's manner of life. 'If we say that we have fellowship with him, and walk in darkness, we lie, and do not the truth: but if we walk in the light, as he is in the light, we have fellowship one with another, and the blood of Jesus Christ his Son cleanseth us from all sin.' How a man or woman 'walks' is how he or she lives from day to day.

To walk in the light is, first of all, to receive and embrace that light by faith. That means to believe on the Name of God's Son, Jesus Christ, and then to act upon one's faith, living in obedience to God's commands, doing the things that please him (1 John 3:22, 23). To walk in darkness is to reject the light, and to go on in the way of sin, the way of the world, the way of 'the wicked one', Satan. To do so is to love darkness and to hate the light (John 3:19-20).

Similarly, John writes of doing the truth (John 3:21; 1 John 1:6). 'Doing the truth' begins with knowing the truth, believing it, and confessing it. If we do not live according to truth from day to day, we show ourselves to be hypocrites and liars, saying one thing and doing another. James 1:22 makes the same point: 'Be ye doers of the word, and not hearers only, deceiving your own selves.'

## The Self-Deceived Walk in Darkness

If we say that we have fellowship with God but walk or live in the darkness of self-centred ungodliness, we deceive ourselves; we live a lie. We live in the realm of the prince of darkness, not in the kingdom of God's dear Son. We have not been born again.

Many people deceive themselves by thinking they are Christians when they are not. Sometimes they are openly living in prolonged, unconfessed sin. Other times they are led astray by false teaching, live by their feelings, love the praise of men, or think that what they do makes them Christians, and so build their salvation apart from Christ's cleansing blood and the godly walk that that salvation produces.

We may deceive ourselves and everyone around us. We think we can deceive God, too, but we cannot, for God always sees us for what we are.

People who say they are Christians but are not drift through life in a haze of self-deception. They do not question or examine themselves; they go on deceived until they come to the last day. Then they will suddenly realize that they have been living in darkness because they hate the light, as Jesus says, 'This is the condemnation, that light is come into the world, and men loved darkness rather than light, because their deeds were evil' (John 3:19). Everyone will 'wake up' at the last day, but those who walk in darkness, like the foolish virgins, will wake up too late to find salvation (Matt. 25:1-13).

## The Christian Walks in the Light

The great human dilemma that confronts all of us is this: If God is light and only the pure in heart will see him (Heb. 12:14), what hope do we have? Haven't we all sinned and come short of the glory of God (Rom. 3:23)? Don't we stand under the righteous judgement of the God of heaven? Doesn't that leave us as undone sinners, forever lost and alone?

God is light, but God also is love (1 John 4:8). The God who is light loves this dark world. He found a way to overcome sin by sending his Son to bear our sin. Jesus Christ opened up a way back to God, taking all our darkness upon himself on Calvary's cross.

If we are to spend eternity with that God in whom there is no darkness, our darkness must be dealt with and conquered. Jesus, the God who is light, became incarnate and entered into darkness on the cross so that by believing in him our darkness would be taken away. His light and his life become ours. That is the great heartbeat of the gospel (cf. 2 Cor. 5:20–21).

A Christian has fellowship with God through Christ's blood (v. 7). The believer walks in the light because of what Jesus did. If we walk in the light, we belong to the kingdom of light. The only way of entrance into that kingdom of light is through the blood of Jesus Christ, God's Son, which cleanses from all sin. Everything in a believer's life is covered by the death of Christ; all sin is put under his blood.

People talk about surrendering something in their life to Christ, or putting it under Christ's blood, as though life was split into various compartments, which God deals with one at a time. But if you are a Christian and you are in fellowship with God, your entire life was covered, once and for all, by the death of Christ. All your sins — past, present, and future — are put under the blood of Christ.

John says that we as Christians must recognize this. True, John goes on to say in verses 8 and 10 that we do not live in this life without sinning, but here he is referring to the kingdom to which we belong. Do we, by Christ's blood, live in the kingdom of light, or do we still live in darkness? Are we under grace, or are our lives still under the dominion of sin (Rom. 6)?

When we come to know God as he truly is, we will be transformed into the likeness of Jesus Christ. We will walk in the light because Christ is the light. The gospel will not simply correct our thinking about God; it will transform our lives into the image and likeness of Christ. That is God's purpose (Rom. 8:29). What is your purpose in life? To be conformed to the likeness of Christ? Are you concerned, not just about being saved, but also about walking in the Light so that you become like Christ?

If you feel alienated from God, run to Christ's blood. Ask him to persuade you that there is no other way to live and meet God than in the light. Ask him to convict you of how dreadful and dangerous it is to live and die in darkness. Do not let the end of your life be recorded for eternity as was the end of Gilbert Tennent (1742–1770). The gravestone of this young man, the son of William Tennent and nephew of Gilbert Tennent, both famous preachers, says:


Here Lies
the mortal part of
GILBERT TENNENT
In the practice of Physick [medicine]
he was
successful and beloved
Young, and in the highest Bloom of life
Death found him
Hopefully in the Lord
But O Reader
Had you heard his last testimony
you would have been convinced
of the extreme madness
of delaying Repentance.

# 4

## *What We Say about Our Sin*

*If we say that we have no sin, we deceive ourselves, and the truth is not in us. If we confess our sins, he is faithful and just to forgive us our sins, and to cleanse us from all unrighteousness. If we say that we have not sinned, we make him a liar, and his word is not in us* (1 John 1:8–10).

In the last verses of 1 John 1, the apostle calls us to examine what we think and say of sin, and what we should do with our sin.

### A Right View of Sin

In 1 John 1:6–10 the Apostle John says four things about our relationship to sin. First, if we walk in the light, the blood of Jesus Christ cleanses us from all sin. This statement refers to the Christian's standing before God. Because we believe on the name of his Son Jesus Christ (1 John 3:23), we are freed from our sins and accounted righteous before God. This justification has been secured by the shedding of Christ's blood to satisfy the demands of God's justice.

Second, John says, 'If we say that we have no sin, we deceive ourselves, and the truth is not in us' (1 John 1:8). This statement refers not to our standing before God, but to what we are by birth and by nature, even as Christians. 'Sin' in this statement refers not to a particular action, but to a power that lives in us in the form of the fallen or depraved nature we have inherited from our first parents. Because the fall into sin involved every part of our human constitution, we speak of 'total depravity'. David spoke as a believer (Ps. 13:8) and a justified sinner (Ps. 32:1-2) when he confessed, 'Behold, I was shapen in iniquity; and in sin did my mother conceive me' (Ps. 51:5). To deny this depravity is to practise self-deception and exchange the truth for a lie, for any other view must be false.

Third, John says, 'If we say that we have not sinned, we make him a liar, and his word is not in us' (1:10). It follows that those burdened with a sinful nature express that nature in particular sins, by thought, word, or deed. Christians are still burdened with such a nature, and they continue to sin. John says that if we deny this, we call God a liar, and reject his Word.

Finally, John says, 'If we confess our sins, he is faithful and just to forgive us our sins, and to cleanse us from all unrighteousness' (1:9). Here John offers real help to Christians — indeed, to anyone burdened with the guilt of particular sins. Guilt and grief need not oppress us. A just and faithful God has appointed a way to obtain his forgiveness, and be cleansed afresh by the blood of Christ.

## Refuting False Views of Sin

In these statements about sin John refutes the Gnostics who claimed to have no sin from which to be cleansed. They denied being sinful by nature, and denied committing actual sins, and therefore had nothing to confess. They considered themselves above sin. They claimed to be 'spiritual ones' (Greek, *pneumatikoi*) who lived on a higher plane. The spiritual experience of enlightenment, the knowledge of mysteries, had elevated them above sin. They claimed that while the human body was evil, the spirit, or essential nature, was good. If they did anything wrong, that was only their flesh doing it, not their real self, their spirit or essential nature; hence they were without sin.

Today, people make similar claims from various perspectives:

- Humanists deny the existence of sin altogether. They say, 'Sin is a physiological aberration, psychological illness, sociological deviation, educational disadvantage, or environmental problem. Man is essentially good. Through education, counseling, medication, social reforms, or economic assistance, he can overcome these problems and will progress until he reaches perfection.' These people are guilty of calling sin by another name, and denying its moral character as an evil power, producing evil fruit.

- Some people admit the possibility of sinning, but deny having a sinful nature. When sins are committed, this must be attributed to some other cause — perhaps a bad example, or negative environmental factors, or even temporary insanity. These people admit that sin exists, but they insist that human nature is nonetheless essentially good. Historically these people came to be called Pelagians, after the name of the theologian, Pelagius, who championed this view.

- Others take the opposite view, admitting to a general human fallibility and proneness to err ('To err is human', as the ancient proverb says) but can't bring themselves to admit to particular sins. Often such people have a distinction in their minds between the gross sins that others may commit and their own 'peccadilloes' or minor sins, which they reckon as counting for little or nothing in the sight of God or man. If they do commit an act gross enough to count for a sin in their eyes, they try to excuse their conduct, blaming someone or something else for their sins, not themselves.

- Antinomians hold that because they are new creatures in Christ, they are no longer depraved, and
  sin cannot be charged to them. They are free to dis-
  pense with the law of God, since that law was made
  for lawless, disobedient sinners.

- Perfectionists admit that man by nature is indeed
  depraved, but by grace he can overcome his depravity altogether. They believe in the possibility of
  Christian perfection, achieved by a rigourous pro-
  gram or method of devotion and good works, or
  else by a special act of the Holy Spirit resulting in
  instant and entire sanctification. This experience is
  sometimes called the baptism of the Spirit, being
  filled with the Spirit, the second blessing, or 'being
  made perfect in love'. John Wesley held such views,
  and they became identified with early Methodism,
  Pentecostalism, and the charismatic movement.

## The Witness of Scripture

Holy Scripture gives a very different account of the matter. As
far back as the days of Noah, 'God saw that the wickedness of
man was great in the earth, and that every imagination of the
thoughts of the heart was only evil continually' (Gen. 6:5). The
great wickedness of man and the violence that filled the earth
in those days (Gen. 6:13) were rooted in the depravity of heart
of all mankind. David bears witness to the fact that things were
no different in his day. In Psalm 14, he says the problem of sin
begins in the folly of man's corrupt heart, expressed in doing
'abominable works'. In fact, 'there is none that doeth good'.
Christ confirms this testimony, saying, 'Out of the heart proceed
evil thoughts, murders, adulteries, fornications, thefts, false witness, blasphemies' (Matt. 15:19).

The person who recognizes the sinful nature of his own
heart does not ask: 'How can someone kill? How can someone
commit adultery? How can someone steal, cheat, or lie?' The

person who knows his own heart knows that the seed of every conceivable sin is within himself. John Bradford, a Puritan preacher, lived near the place where criminals were tied behind a cart, then taken to be hung on the gallows. As Bradford saw the condemned men walk past his door, he would say, 'There goes John Bradford, but for the grace of God.'

There are several consequences of denying what Scripture says about our sinful nature, and the sins we commit. First, we deceive ourselves. We believe a lie of our own making. In other words, we refuse to see ourselves as we truly are, and as God sees us. Since God's Word is truth (John 17:17), any view that conflicts with that Word must be false.

Self-deception is tragic because it is self-destructive. The person who deceives himself goes on in his error, unaware that anything is wrong. He does not examine himself. He never asks, 'What must I do to be saved?' Isaiah paints the portrait of such a man: 'He feedeth on ashes: a deceived heart hath turned him aside, that he cannot deliver his soul, nor say, Is there not a lie in my right hand?' (Isa. 44:20).

The second consequence of denying our sinful nature is that 'the truth is not in us'. So long as we fill our hearts with a lie of our own making, we have no room in our hearts for God's truth. We close our minds to the light, and we harden our hearts. In a state of self-deception, we will drift on until the Last Day, when we will discover all too late that the truth is not in us.

Third, John says, 'If we say that we have not sinned, we make him [God] a liar, and his word is not in us' (1:10). When we say we have not sinned, we are saying that God is bearing false witness, since he said in his Word, 'All have sinned and come short of the glory of God' (Rom 3:23), and 'There is none righteous, no, not one' (Rom. 3:10).

Fourth, we make the cross of Jesus Christ of no account. Christianity teaches that 'the wrath of God against sin is so great, that rather than it should go unpunished, he hath punished the same in the his beloved Son Jesus Christ with the bitter and shameful death of the cross' ('Form for the Administration of the Lord's Supper', *The Psalter,* p.136). If we have no sin, and have not sinned, then why did Christ go to the cross? Why this outpouring of righteous anger, this punishment, this bitter and shameful death?

When we deny our sins, we deceive our selves, and the truth is not in us. We make God a liar, and his Word is not in us. We mock God's truth, the cross of Calvary, and the face of divine love that shines upon us from Calvary. Christ himself, the incarnate Word of life, is not in us. We are cut off from eternal life.

## When We Confess Our Sins

If our eyes have been opened to see ourselves and our sins for what they truly are in God's sight, what must we do? What is the alternative to denial? John holds forth this great promise: 'If we confess our sins, he is faithful and just to forgive us our sins, and to cleanse us from all unrighteousness' (1:9).

The word *confess* (Greek, *homologeo*) literally means 'to agree with' and 'to say the same thing'. Implicit in the word itself is the fact that God has spoken to us by his servants the prophets, by his Son Jesus Christ, and by Christ's servants, the apostles and the ministers of the Word, who preach 'repentance toward God and faith toward our Lord Jesus Christ' (Acts 20:21). Confession is our heartfelt response to what God has shown us by his Word and Spirit. When we confess our sins, therefore, it means we have the same view of our sins as God has. We agree with God that we have sinned against him by breaking his commandments.

Confession of sins makes us see ourselves in light of the living God and his holy law. We stop comparing ourselves to others. We stop commending ourselves. We stop excusing ourselves, or blaming others. Instead, we confess that we are sinners and deserve to be punished. We say 'amen' to God's guilty verdict on our lives. We see the heinousness of sin. We agree with God that sin will damn us to everlasting hell unless he forgives and cleanses us.

Confession is personal. We each confess our own sins to God. There are times when we have wronged someone and must confess our sin to that person. Jesus said if we come to the altar and remember that our brother has something against us, we must first go and be reconciled to the brother. Then we may come to God and offer him our sacrifice (Matt. 18:15). Still, ultimately, all sin is sin against God (Ps. 51:4; cf. 2 Sam. 12:13).

Confession of sins is also corporate, as John's use of the plural indicates. It is part of corporate Christian prayer. Christ taught his disciples to pray, 'Forgive us our debts' (Matt. 6:12). Confession of sins has been a part of the public worship of the church under both testaments. If God's children had no sin, and did not sin, not one of the penitential Psalms (Pss. 6, 32, 38, 51, 102, 130, 143) would have been written, for all were composed by holy men of God, and appointed for the use of the visible church and all her members.

Too often we believers ignore the evidence of sin in our lives. That is like ignoring the warning light on the dashboard of your car that says, 'Check oil'. If we fail to check the oil, something bad may happen to the car. Likewise, if we do not confess our sins daily, we will find ourselves in deep spiritual trouble. Confession of sins is an urgent matter. 'Keep short accounts with God.'

## God's Response to Confession

What happens when we confess our sins? John does not leave us in doubt. He declares that God 'is faithful and just to forgive us our sins, and to cleanse us from all unrighteousness'. There are three aspects to God's forgiveness, John says:

1.  God is *faithful* to forgive us. God is true to his character and to his Word. The psalmist declares, 'If thou, LORD, shouldest mark iniquities, O LORD, who shall stand? But there is forgiveness with thee, that thou mayest be feared ... Let Israel hope in the LORD for with the LORD there is mercy, and with him is plenteous redemption' (Ps. 130:3,4,7). That this is God's character comes to expression in the gospel promise of the forgiveness of

sins made to all who believe on the name of his Son
Jesus Christ.

2.  God is *just* to forgive us. Having punished sin in the
    person of his beloved Son Jesus Christ with the bitter
    and shameful death of the cross, he is free to forgive
    our sins, thus showing mercy to sinners without doing
    any injury to his perfect justice. If you are a believer,
    your comfort is that Jesus stood in your guilty place,
    bearing your load, removing your guilt, cancelling your
    debt, and nailing your curse to his cross. He took your
    punishment to the grave and buried it there forever.

    When we come to God and confess our sins, God
    promises that because of what Jesus has done on the
    cross, he will forgive our sins. Indeed, if Jesus took our
    sins to the cross of Calvary and God did not forgive us,
    God would no longer be just. He would be demanding
    a double payment for our sin. The wonderful news of
    the gospel is that Jesus paid it all. God executed his
    justice on Christ so that he might administer his full and
    free forgiveness to you as a penitent, believing sinner.
    Through faith in Christ, your sin — past, present, and
    future — can be forgiven.

3.  God *cleanses* us from all unrighteousness. Here some-
    thing is added to forgiveness. Forgiveness is God's act
    of justification, freeing us from our sins and accounting
    us righteous before him, for Jesus' sake. Cleansing is
    God's work of sanctification, washing us from our sins
    in Christ's blood, and renewing us by the power of the
    Holy Spirit. The unfolding or progressive work of sanc-
    tification follows upon the definitive act of justification.
    Both are the work of God in us, the God who forgives
    all our sins and cleanses us from all unrighteousness.

## Daily Cleansing

God promises us continued cleansing from all unrighteousness. Because we sin daily, and we must live day by day with our remaining depravity and all its evil fruits, we need daily forgiveness and cleansing. We need to close the breach that our sins make in our communion with God. We need to find healing for the hurt we inflict on ourselves and on our fellow human beings. We need to deal with each day's accumulation of debts. Every day we must confess our sins to God, seeking that forgiveness and cleansing he alone can bestow.

This is true for every Christian, and especially for those who may have wandered far from the paths of righteousness and life. By the grace of the Holy Spirit, we must retrace our steps. We must return to Christ, whose blood cleanses from all sin, and to God, who is faithful and just to forgive our sins and cleanse us from all unrighteousness.

# 5

# *Propitiation for Sin*

*My little children, these things write I unto you, that ye sin not. And if any man sin, we have an advocate with the Father, Jesus Christ the righteous: and he is the propitiation for our sins: and not for ours only, but also for the sins of the whole world* (1 John 2:1-2).

First John 2:1-2 holds the answer to the false teaching of the Gnostics in John's day and every needy sinner in our day is. We still sin after we become believers, John says, but God has made perfect provision for our sin. God has not left us hopeless; he has provided someone to help us. We have Jesus Christ the righteous, who speaks to the Father in our behalf.

When you hire an attorney today, he or she is usually a professional. In New Testament times, you would have asked your best friend to be your advocate. That friend's appearing with you and speaking for you was a proof of true friendship. The word for advocate in 1 John 2:1 is *paracletos*. If we are believers, we have a *paracletos* with the Father, Jesus Christ the righteous, our best friend and advocate whom we call on to come alongside to help us.

Do you have an advocate with the Father? Does Christ plead your cause before the judgement seat of God in heaven? Or do you think that you can argue your own defence? Will you be compelled to stand alone (Ps. 13:1-2)?

## Payment for Our Sin

What does Christ our advocate say to the Father on our behalf? What is his line of defence? Does he say, 'Father, these people are innocent'? That would be a lie. Does he excuse our sin, saying, 'Father, there are extenuating circumstances'? Does he plead leniency because of ignorance — does he say that we were trapped into sin and did not know what we were doing? That, too, would be a lie — we have a conscience!

John sheds light on these questions in verse 2 where he says that Jesus Christ is the propitiation for our sins. 'Propitiate' means to appease or atone; hence, 'propitiation' appeases or atones. If you anger someone, you make propitiation for your offence in one way or another to appease him. You offer a peace offering so that your guilt is atoned for and your relationship can be restored.

In our relationship with God, Christ's propitiation addressed the wrath of God; it quenched the terrible fire of his burning anger. Jesus Christ is the propitiation that delivered us from God's anger against us by taking it on himself. His death was the once-for-all propitiation. His further ministry of intercession applies that propitiation. Even now, Jesus stands before his Father, acknowledging the guilt and judgement that we deserve. Then he, in essence, shows his pierced hands and feet and wounded side, and says, as it were, 'Father, I have paid the price of their sin. These marks testify that I have suffered the wrath and the judgement that their sin deserved.'

Whether Jesus literally speaks such words as these, no one knows. Some theologians reason that this is in essence what he does, though he says nothing literally, as that is not needed, since he himself is our defence. One thing is sure: If we are believers, Christ is our advocate with the Father however that may take place. He stands before the Father, pleading our defence. Because God has executed his righteous wrath upon his Son in our place, he will not demand payment of us. That is why true believers can say:

*My hope is built on nothing less,*
*Than Jesus' blood and righteousness.*

Jesus Christ's defence before God is so complete that it is sufficient for the sins of the world. As John says, 'Not for ours only, but also for the sins of the whole world' (2:2). John is speaking here of Christian believers — those who have seen themselves lost before God and who have put their hope in Jesus Christ as God's loving provision for their sin.

By 'whole world' John is also saying that the sacrifice Christ made was not only for the Jews or for a small group of first-century believers but for people of every tribe, tongue, and nation through all time. John Murray speaks about the 'ethnic universalism' of the gospel, meaning that those for whom Christ died are spread among all nations.

Believers have a worldwide Advocate with the Father. Could there be anything more glorious than that? When Satan threatens to undo us, saying, 'How can you call yourself a Christian? Look at your life!', point to Christ and say, 'He has paid the price of all my sin. His blood and righteousness cover me before God.' When God's holy law accuses us of breaking the commandments, point to Christ and say:

*When Satan tempts me to despair,*
*And tells me of the guilt within;*
*Upwards I look and see him there,*
*Who put an end to all my sin.*

When our hearts condemn us, we lay our hearts before Christ, and confess with Charles Spurgeon, 'Sinner as I am, and never more consciously so than I am now that God's Spirit has enlightened me, I yet know that if any man sin we have an Advocate with the Father, and I, black, foul, and filthy, more foul and filthy than I ever thought myself to be, put my case into the hand of my Advocate, and leave it there for ever' (*Metropolitan Tabernacle Pulpit*, 9:346).

Our advocate with the Father is the Father's only-begotten Son who is also one with the Father. The Father says to this

Advocate, 'Ask of me and I will give you the ends of the earth for your inheritance. I will give you whatever you plead' (cf. Ps. 2:8; John 11:42).

John Calvin said it like this: 'The reason why God does not impute our sins to us is because he looks on Christ the Intercessor, and he sees there the marks of redemption — that for all for whom he died the price has been paid.'

## The Consequences of Forgiveness

There are no limitations on forgiveness. The consequences of such forgiveness for us are far-reaching and life-transforming: 'My little children, these things write I unto you, that ye sin not' (1 John 2:1). Speaking tenderly to believers as 'little children', John stresses that God's purpose for those who believe in Jesus Christ and whose sins are washed away in his blood is that we no longer sin. The Gnostics treated sin lightly, saying their superior knowledge elevated them so that what was sin for others was no longer sin for them.

God does not treat sin that way. As a heavenly sculptor, God starts with a large block of human marble, then begins cutting into it to remove every blemish and flaw. He does that so he can create something glorious. All of God's work in the world is directed to saving sinners and eradicating sin in them. If we are believers, he no longer counts our sin against us in Christ. Though we still sin, yet happily, God sets his heart on removing sin completely from our lives.

We need to know this to make sense of the work of Jesus Christ. Jesus did not come into the world only to save us from hell and to bring us to heaven. He did not come only to forgive our sins. He came also to make us like himself. He came to both justify and sanctify us.

When John writes, 'These things write I unto you, that ye sin not', understand that God's purpose is to conform Christian believers to the likeness of his Son. In Romans 8:29, Paul repeats this thought, saying that God has predestined sinners to be conformed to the likeness of his Son. God's ultimate purpose is to so eradicate sin from our lives that we will be replicas of his Son, the firstborn among many brethren.

When a farmer sows his seed, he does not say, 'My work is over.' His work has only begun. He has sown the seed, but what he has in mind is the harvest that the seed will produce. So the farmer watches over his seed, fertilizing and watering it. Likewise, when God plants the seed of new life in our hearts, he lovingly tends it so that we might ultimately be transformed in heart and mind and life and be conformed to the God of light.

The true believer aims high, John says. His goal is not to sin at all. No doubt you have heard the expression, 'Aim at nothing and you will hit it every time.' Likewise, if you aim at something less than perfection, you will certainly achieve it. You might object, saying, 'Yes, but if I aim at perfection, I will not achieve that, either. Why try reaching for a goal that I know I cannot accomplish? Goals should be achievable.'

If you do not firmly determine to break with sin, you will have little success in overcoming sin in your life. Sin should be abhorrent to you. We will not reach perfection this side of eternity, of course. As long as we are in the body, we sin. We grieve God and one another with our sin. But one of the great marks of a genuine Christian is that once the seed of new life is planted within him, he has a new attitude to sin. He begins to see sin for what it is, viewing it as so heinous that it nailed the Son of God to a cross and moved God to abandon his Son. The believer longs to be free of sin so that he might love God purely for who he is and for what he has done.

There is a remarkable mix of joy and sorrow in the believer. The believer rejoices in Christ and all that Christ has done, yet he also cries, 'O wretched man that I am! who shall deliver me from the body of this death?' (Rom. 7:24). Like Paul, the believer looks forward to the great day when he will receive a heavenly body that is completely conformed to Christ.

If you are not a true child of God, ask yourself, how shall I become just with God? Stop denying that you live in the sphere of sin and are full of sin. Confess your sin and trust God to cleanse you from all unrighteousness by the propitiating blood

of the Lord Jesus Christ. Cast away all your self-commenda-
tions and receive Christ as a needy sinner. Go to him just as
you are. God will not cast away any sinner who comes to him,
for, 'If any man sin, we have an advocate with the Father, Jesus
Christ the righteous.'

# 6

## *Assurance of Faith*

*And hereby we do know that we know him, if we keep his commandments. He that saith, I know him, and keepeth not his commandments, is a liar, and the truth is not in him. But whoso keepeth his word, in him verily is the love of God perfected: hereby know we that we are in him. He that saith he abideth in him ought himself also so to walk, even as he walked* (1 John 2:3–6).

A Christian with assurance of faith knows that he belongs to Christ, that his sins are forgiven, that God loves him, and that he will enjoy everlasting salvation. If a person does not have this assurance, how can he get it? In these verses, John begins to answer these questions. He continues to develop the theme of assurance throughout the remainder of the epistle.

Notice how John begins in verse 3: 'And hereby we do know that we know him'. John assumes that it is normal for Christians to be assured of their salvation. He is persuaded that God's people should have at least some degree of assurance.

### The Essence of Assurance

For John's readers, the problem of assurance was related to the influence of Gnostic prophets. The Gnostics claimed to have assurance but their assurance was spurious. These false prophets

were questioning the authenticity of the faith of believers, saying, in effect, 'You cannot be real Christians because you have
not experienced what we have experienced. We have been enlightened. We have been initiated into the deep things of God.
You do not know what we know.'

Claiming superiority of faith has been a problem throughout the centuries and is still with us today. It is evident in people
who say, 'If you are not in my church, you cannot be a real
Christian', as if their church has a monopoly on Christian truth.
It is evident in people who say, 'If you have not experienced the
special blessing that I have had, you cannot have assurance.'
Today, some people say this about receiving the baptism of the
Spirit, speaking in tongues, and being 'slain in the Spirit'. Like
the Gnostics in John's day, they make people who have not
had such experiences feel inferior in the faith or even doubt that
they are Christians at all.

John does not want people to take assurance of faith lightly,
however. Even though the Gnostics are wrong, it is possible
that people who assume they are believers have never truly believed. People may claim that they know Christ, but do they
possess a genuinely biblical, experiential knowledge? John and
the other apostles regard this as a significant question for people
to answer.

*We Know Him*

In 1 John 2:3–6, John offers three dimensions of Christian assurance. The first dimension of assurance John mentions is that
we know Christ personally and intimately: 'Hereby we do know
that we know him' (v. 3). Scripture uses the term *knowing* in
the sense of personal and intimate knowledge. We are to know
Christ in the following ways:

1. *By believing in Christ.* Scripture says that salvation is
   rooted in the saving knowledge of Jesus Christ. Jesus
   says in his high-priestly prayer in John 17, 'This is life
   eternal, that they might know thee, the only true God,
   and Jesus Christ whom thou hast sent' (v. 3).

'To know' and 'to believe' are often nearly synonymous in Scripture. Knowing and believing in Christ
was Paul's consolation when he wrote to Timothy from
prison, 'For the which cause I also suffer these things:
nevertheless I am not ashamed: for I know whom I have
believed, and am persuaded that he is able to keep that
which I have committed unto him against that day'
(2 Tim. 1:12). Notice that Paul does not say, 'I know
*about* the One in whom I have believed.' Paul knows
the Person in whom he believes. Paul goes on to say, 'I
am *persuaded* that he is able to keep that which I have
committed unto him against that day.' Paul speaks with
assurance. He knows that he knows.

2. *By experiencing Christ.* Scripture says that Christ 'knew
   no sin', meaning that Christ never experienced sin. To
   know Christ means to experience the redeeming power
   of his saving grace in granting us his righteousness and
   in conquering our sins. It means experiencing Christ
   through his offices, natures, states, and benefits.

   The Apostle Paul experienced Christ as the essence
   and goal of his entire life. 'I count all things but loss
   for the excellency of the knowledge of Christ Jesus
   my Lord', he says, and then adds that he yearns to be
   found in Christ that he 'may know him and the power
   of his resurrection, and the fellowship of his sufferings'
   (Phil. 3:8, 10). This kind of knowledge does not come
   from mere observation or instruction. We need an experiential knowledge of being crucified and raised with
   Christ.

3. *By communing with Christ.* In Job 22:21, Eliphaz says,
   'Acquaint now thyself with him.' This kind of acquaintance means having the kind of established relationship
   that allows constant access to each other. It signifies
   freedom to converse with each other. When the Bible
   speaks about knowing Jesus, it means having communion with him, enjoying his presence, and hearing his

voice through his Word. It means unburdening one's soul before Christ and speaking to him through prayer and praise.

*We Are in Him*

The second dimension of assurance of faith is knowing that we are personally united to Christ. John says, 'He that saith, I know him, and keepeth not his commandments, is a liar, and the truth is not in him. But whoso keepeth his word, in him verily is the love of God perfected: hereby know we that we are in him' (2:4-5).

When we are born again through the power of the Holy Spirit, we are personally united with Jesus Christ. John uses the words *in him* four times in four verses. Paul, too, does not tire of describing a Christian this way. I once counted 164 places in Paul's epistles in which Paul uses this phrase or a similar one — *in Christ, in Christ Jesus,* or *in him.* Paul loves to describe the Christian as being in Christ. 'If any man be *in Christ*, he is a new creature', Paul says in 2 Corinthians 5:17. In Romans 8:1 he says, 'There is therefore now no condemnation to them which are *in Christ Jesus,* who walk not after the flesh, but after the Spirit.' And, in Galatians 3:26 he says, 'For ye are all the children of God by faith *in Christ Jesus.*'

The Spirit is in Christ first of all; hence, assurance means knowing that if the Spirit is in us, Christ is in us, and we are in Christ. That assured knowledge of being united to Christ is usually a growth process that results from being increasingly anchored in the person and work of Christ by Word-centred saving faith.

*We Abide in Him*

The third dimension of assurance consists of abiding in Christ: 'He that saith he abideth in him ought himself also so to walk, even as he walked' (v. 6). John says here that we may be assured that we are Christians if we abide in Christ, for abiding in

Christ proves that we are in union and communion with him. As believers, our claim to abide in Christ is proven by 'walking as Christ walked'. Christ abides in us — that is his promise. We abide in him — that is our duty.

True acquaintance with our Lord Jesus Christ is not momentary. It is not merely a profession made years ago. It is not something that depends on periodic religious experiences, as confirming and helpful as they may be. Knowing Christ and abiding in him is a relationship that must develop and grow.

John 15 teaches us that as a branch draws its life from its vine, the branch grows and bears fruit by abiding in the vine. Likewise, Jesus says in verse 6 that if a man professes to be a Christian but does not abide in Christ, his profession is meaningless. He becomes a withered, dry branch good only for burning.

The essence of Christian assurance, then, is knowing that we know Jesus Christ personally — knowing that we are personally united to him and knowing that we abide in him day by day. Christianity cannot be reduced to a decision we made in the past. True Christianity is the progression of a life linked to Jesus Christ. If we do not know this, and if we do not know that we know it, then we lack assurance of faith.

## The Evidence of Assurance

Running parallel with the three dimensions of the essence of Christian assurance, John expounds three evidences of assurance. Those who are personally know, are united with, and abide in Jesus, will manifest these evidences.

### Obedience to the Law of God

The first evidence for assurance of salvation is obedience to the moral law of God. John says, 'Hereby we do know that we know him, if we keep his commandments. He that saith, I know him, and keepeth not his commandments, is a liar, and the truth is not in him' (vv. 3-4). A person can have wonderful experiences and feelings and can make many claims, but if he does not obey God's law, he is a liar. He does not know what he claims to know.

When Christ saves a sinner, Christ's presence becomes evident in how that person obeys God's commands. We know that we know Christ and that he has begotten us into his family if we obey his commands.

The practical evidence of authentic God-given faith is a new lifestyle that reflects a different orientation spiritually and emotionally. A believer is no longer shaped by the thinking, opinions, and values of this world but by the commandments of God. When Christ comes into a sinner's life, he grants the loving desire to embrace the commandments of God.

The proof of love is loyalty, John says. You know that someone truly loves a person not by the fine words he says, but by how he treats the person he loves. We all need to hear that we are loved. Some of us should express love more often, but it is even more important to show someone that you love him. True love desires to please the loved one. That desire is best expressed by the way you treat a person, showing how much you prize and cherish him or her. Similarly, John says, 'We know that we know God', first and foremost, 'if we keep his commandments'. Active obedience is the first expression of true love for God.

When a believer obeys God from the heart, and the Spirit testifies to that in his conscience (Rom. 8:15-16), the believer may conclude that he is a child of God. By God's grace, he lovingly keeps God's commandments and clings to them with reverence. The believer is right to conclude that God's grace is at work in his life. God shows the believer that his earnest desire to fulfil God's commandments, and his actual obeying of them, is all of God's grace.

It is impossible to maintain high levels of assurance when we exercise low levels of obedience. Spurgeon rightly said, 'The lack of practical obedience to Christ is the root of 999 of every 1000 of our doubts and fears.'

Assurance is a gracious privilege that God sometimes removes from his people when they do not walk in obedience

before him. The withdrawal of assurance is actually beneficial
for believers, for it shows them the disastrous fruits of disobedience. It convinces them to repent afresh of their sin, to vow to
obey God by his grace, and to plead with God to restore the joy
of his salvation. As one theologian says, 'You had better lose
your assurance when you walk in disobedience.'

Two important truths about obedience must be emphasized
here: First, no one keeps God's commands perfectly. Only Jesus
perfectly obeyed the law. We cannot keep God's commands
perfectly, but we can keep them purposefully. We can rise each
day with longing in our heart to do what is in accordance with
God's will. We can pray, 'Lord, not my will but thy will be done.
Shape me today by the Word that thou hast spoken, even in a
world that repudiates thee.'

Second, there are two kinds of obedience. *Legal obedience*
says, 'If I obey God, he will be good to me.' That attitude shows
that we do not truly believe the gospel promise, for we can do
nothing to make God gracious to us. We could as soon climb
to the moon on a rope of sand or to the sun on a rope of ice
than make God gracious to us by our obedience. Our obedience is sporadic and partial at best. Legal obedience is exemplified in the prodigal son's elder brother, who said, 'Lo, these
many years do I serve thee, neither transgressed I at any time
thy commandment' (Luke 15:29). Legal obedience does not
move beyond a sense of duty.

*Evangelical obedience* says, 'God loved me and gave his
Son for me. He saved me, forgave me, and adopted me into
his family. It is my newfound joy and desire to obey him — not
to win anything from him — but to express my love for all that
he has done for me.' The source of God-pleasing obedience
is Christ. What prompts our hearts to evangelical obedience is
being gripped by the gospel; such obedience says, 'The Son of
God did everything for me. The least I can do to thank him is to
obey his commands.'

Are we motivated by evangelical obedience? Do we want to
do everything that Christ has commanded us to do? Or do we
say, 'We love Jesus. He is precious to us. That is enough. The
commandments are not important'?

John warns us: 'He that saith, I know him, and keepeth not his commandments, is a liar, and the truth is not in him' (v. 4). A person lies if he says he knows Christ when he really does not. He lies doctrinally, because he promotes the heresy that those who live perpetually in sin can truly know the Saviour. He lies practically, because he acts like he knows the truth but his life shows that he does not. He is a stranger to the truth.

*Adherence to the Word of God*

John says in verse 5, 'But whoso keepeth his word, in him verily is the love of God perfected: hereby know we that we are in him.' John takes obedience to God's law a step farther by speaking about adherence to the Word of God. 'Whoso keepeth his word' means 'He who adheres to, or holds on to my doctrine and my teaching'.

When Jesus told the parable of the sower of seeds into different soils, the last soil he spoke of was good ground. The seed that fell into good ground brought forth much fruit. Jesus said the good ground represented those 'which in an honest and good heart, having heard the word, keep it, and bring forth fruit with patience' (Luke 8:15). Likewise, John says that a Christian is assured of salvation if he receives the Word of God, holds on to it, and strives to live according to that Word.

John adds something astonishing: 'whoso keepeth his word, in him verily is the love of God perfected' (v. 5). If someone adheres to God's Word gladly from the heart, God's love is perfected in him. 'To perfect' here means 'to accomplish, to complete, or to bring to the goal proposed'. John is saying, 'In this person God's love accomplishes its purpose.'

We long to be overwhelmed by the love of God, and by God's grace, we may experience that, for as John says, 'The love of God is perfected' in those who adhere to God's Word. There is a link between gladly embracing God's Word and experiencing the fulness of God's love in our lives.

All of this contrasts with turning away from the Word to embrace unbiblical teachings and corrupt practices. Those who do so embrace 'another gospel' (2 Cor. 11:4); the love of God is not perfected in them, for they are not in Christ. Here, then, is a foundational mark of grace by which we must examine ourselves: Do we adhere to the Word of God? Do we cling to this Word, and strive to know and keep it better? Do we search and love the Scriptures and yearn to live in accord with them? Truthful answers to these questions reveal whether or not the love of God is perfected in us.

## Walking as Jesus Walked

The third evidence of salvation, according to John, is that he who 'abideth in him ought himself also so to walk, even as he walked'. A Christian is united with Christ and partakes of all of Christ's blessings and benefits. Like a branch being grafted into a tree, the branch slowly becomes part of the tree, and the life of the tree flows into the branch. John 15:5 says, 'I am the vine, ye are the branches: he that abideth in me, and I in him, the same bringeth forth much fruit: for without me ye can do nothing.'

If a branch is truly united to the tree, it possesses the same life as the tree and brings forth the same fruit as the tree. That is precisely the point John makes when he says, 'Hereby know we that we are in him. He that saith he abideth in him ought himself also so to walk, even as he walked.' If we truly are Christ's, it will be evident in how our life conforms to Christ's life. If we are *in* Christ, we will be *like* Christ.

Walking as Christ did means the following:

1. *Making Jesus' priorities your own by faith.* Walking implies action, direction, and purpose. Jesus says in John 6:38, 'For I came down from heaven, not to do mine own will, but the will of him that sent me.' The greatest priority of Jesus' life was not doing his own will but that of his Father.

2. *Delighting in God's law.* Jesus loved God's law and kept it. God's Word was his delight. Even when he was twelve years old, Jesus wanted to be in the house of

God, discussing the Word of God. That was what he most delighted to do (Ps. 40:8).

3. *Having compassion for others.* Jesus had a servant's heart in caring for the needs of others. When Jesus washed his disciples' feet, he told them, 'I have given you an example, that ye should do as I have done to you' (John 13:15). Jesus came not to be served, but to serve. Likewise, we must live for others rather than ourselves. How do you view others — as a pull on your time, an inconvenience, a disruption, or as people in need of a loving, encouraging word?

4. *Repaying evil with good.*    First Peter 2:23 tells us that Jesus refused to repay evil with evil. It says that Jesus, 'when he was reviled, reviled not again; when he suffered, he threatened not; but committed himself to him that judgeth righteously'. Instead of repaying evil with evil, Jesus said of his unrighteous judges and executioners, 'Father, forgive them; for they know not what they do' (Luke 23:34).
   How do we respond when people do bad things to us? Do we vow, 'I'll get even with you, no matter how long it takes'? Or do we forgive the offence and pray for the person who wronged us?

5. *Acting in love.* If you wish to see love personified, look at Christ. Jesus loved little children and welcomed them even when others considered them an intrusion. Jesus loved widows and healed their sick children. He loves sinners of every type, draws them to himself, and invites them to cast all their needs and sins upon him. Above all, Jesus loves his Father.

You may shrink at the thought of comparing yourself with Jesus. You are too aware of sin and shortcomings in your life to make such a claim. Yet is there within you a small beginning of obedience, of Christ-likeness? Is your life bent toward Christ?

The great predestinating purpose of God is to conform his people to the likeness of his Son (Rom. 8:29). That is what God is doing through the church — taking people and reshaping them into the likeness of his Son. He reshapes people by working in them that which is pleasing in his sight: obedience to his commandments, adherence to his Word, and walking as Jesus walked.

# 7

# *The Test of Love*

*Brethren, I write no new commandment unto you, but an old commandment which ye had from the beginning. The old commandment is the word which ye have heard from the beginning. Again, a new commandment I write unto you, which thing is true in him and in you: because the darkness is past, and the true light now shineth. He that saith he is in the light, and hateth his brother, is in darkness even until now. He that loveth his brother abideth in the light, and there is none occasion of stumbling in him. But he that hateth his brother is in darkness, and walketh in darkness, and knoweth not whither he goeth, because that darkness hath blinded his eyes* (1 John 2:7–11).

In these verses John presents brotherly love as another test for self-examination. We have already considered the test of obedience (2:3-6). Now, John moves to a second test — the test of love. He will move on to three more tests: the test of experiential faith (2:12–14), the test of rejecting worldliness (2:15–17), and the test of sound faith (2:18–29). The Gnostics and other unbelievers fail all five tests. By grace, the true Christian passes all of them.

In many ways, loving one another is the crucial test of Christian faith. Such love involves cherishing and valuing others, doing good to others, and seeking the best welfare of others, without thought of receiving love in return. John stresses this theme throughout his epistle because he knows there can be no real fellowship among believers if they have no love for one another.

## An Old Commandment Made New

First, notice that John speaks about the commandment of love. 'Brethren, I write no new commandment unto you, but an old commandment which ye had from the beginning', John says. 'The old commandment is the word which ye have heard from the beginning. Again, a new commandment I write unto you, which thing is true in him and in you: because the darkness is past, and the true light now shineth' (2:7–8). At first glance, John appears to be speaking of different commandments here — an old and a new one. But when you look at these verses carefully and compare them with other Scriptures, it becomes evident that John speaks of one commandment with old and new dimensions. It is an old commandment that was given long before, but it now has received another emphasis so that it appears altogether new.

John says in verse 7 that this commandment was proclaimed before. His readers have heard this commandment from the beginning, meaning they have known it from the beginning of their Christian experience. From the time they were first introduced to the gospel, they have been commanded to love one another. But in another, more important sense, the entire church of God throughout its history has received this commandment. In John 13:34–35, Jesus declared, 'A new commandment I give unto you, That ye love one another; as I have loved you, that ye also love one another. By this shall all men know that ye are my disciples, if ye have love to one another.' In John 15:12 and 17, Jesus added, 'This is my commandment, That ye love one another, as I have loved you … These things I command you, that ye love one another.'

This commandment was already known in the Old Testament period. In summarizing the law, Jesus drew from Deuteronomy

6:5 when he said, 'Thou shalt love the Lord thy God with all thy heart, and with all thy soul, and with all thy mind. This is the first and great commandment. And the second is like unto it, Thou shalt love thy neighbour as thyself' (Matt. 22:37, 40).

So it was an old commandment; but John goes on to describe it as new: 'Again, a new commandment I write unto you, which thing is true in him [i.e., Jesus Christ] and in you.' This old commandment has a new emphasis, John says, because of how it has been fulfilled in Christ and in those who believe in him.

Jesus demonstrated throughout his life love to his Father and to others. Consider how he responded to the little band of disciples that followed him. How they tried him with their unbelief and stubbornness and slowness. Though he grew weary of that at times, Jesus patiently showed love to his followers, even to Peter who would deny him and Judas who would betray him.

Through Christ, the commandment to love acquired a deeper meaning. Jesus said, 'I am the good shepherd; the good shepherd lays down his life for his sheep.' He so loved his brothers and sisters that he was willing to die for them. He loved them all the way to the cross of Calvary.

John goes on to say that this love is not only evident in Christ, but 'in you' (v. 8) — that is, in believers who have been born again of the Spirit. John writes to reassure Christians who may feel inferior because they do not have the great wisdom and experiences that the Gnostics claim to have. 'I have seen the transformation of God in your lives', John says to these believers. 'I have seen that command begin to take root in you. Be encouraged.'

True Christians understand what this old, yet new commandment means. They have learned how faith changes their relationships with others. Why? Because in coming to know the love of God, believers begin to reflect God's love in their relationships with others. Having seen God's love for them, they reflect that love to others.

John goes on to say that this love can be exercised 'because the darkness is past, and the true light now shineth' (v. 8b). Just as Jesus came to dispel the darkness of the old dispensation of types and shadows and to bring the light of the love and grace of God to sinners, so darkness begins to pass away in a believer and true light begins to shine. The light and love of God enable the regenerated person to love God and to show something of God's love to others.

God calls Christians to love one another as Christ loves us. The cross reveals the depth of the Saviour's love for us; the new command is to reflect that love to each other in this fallen, sinful world. As 1 John 3:16 says, 'Hereby perceive we the love of God, because he laid down his life for us: and we ought to lay down our lives for the brethren.'

When the New Testament speaks of brotherly love, it is not speaking about merely a sympathetic heart or a kindly disposition or even a willingness to give up something to help someone else. It is speaking about self-sacrifice, servanthood — a 'washing of the saints' feet', and a readiness to die for the everlasting good of others.

This is the new emphasis that has come with Jesus Christ, our Saviour. The Father looks at his children and says, 'Love one another, whatever you do.' By that he does not mean indulge one another, be sentimental toward one another, or turn a blind eye to each other's sin. He means that we must so love others that we are willing to die for a brother or sister's good. Oh, that Christ could say of us as John says of the believers to whom he wrote, 'I see this new command in you. I see that you are even willing to die, if need be, for the brethren's sake!'

**Teachers Tested by This Command**

John now applies the test of love to teachers who fail to exhibit such love. Undoubtedly John is referring here to the Gnostics who were troubling true believers by making them feel inferior as Christians. The Gnostics claimed to have great light, but their lives didn't match their profession. They did not love all those who professed Christ. So John says in verse 9, 'He that saith he is in the light, and hateth his brother, is in darkness even until now.'

John is reaffirming what Paul says in 1 Thessalonians 4:9, 'But as touching brotherly love ye need not that I write unto you: for ye yourselves are taught of God to love one another.' In other words, if you have received the light of God, you will want to love one another because God prompts you to do that. You don't need someone to tell you that.

John expands that teaching here, saying that you cannot say that you love God if you do not love your brother or sister in the church. If you do not love your brother or sister in Christ, that proves that you do not love God. As John says, 'He that saith he is in the light, and hateth his brother, is in darkness even unto now.' This strong statement condemns the faith of Gnostic teachers and squares with what Jesus' teaching that he who loves Jesus, keeps his commandments.

### The True and False Revealed

John presents two case studies. First, he presents the Christian whose testimony proves true when tested by the commandment to love: 'He that loveth his brother abideth in the light, and there is none occasion of stumbling in him' (v. 10).

This Christian, who knows the grace of God in his life and who lives in the light of Christ, loves his brother — his brother in the flesh, his spiritual brother, his neighbour-brother, and his brother at work and school. He does not love his brother's sins, but he loves his brother and his soul. As such, the Christian wants what is best for his brother.

The true Christian 'abides in the light', meaning he lives continually in obedience to the commandment to love. He lives continually in the Word and in Christ. He has not only been brought into the light; he wants to continue living in the light. If he falls into sin, particularly in his relationships with others, he will strive to get back into the light. He cannot tolerate being in the darkness. That is the mark of the true Christian: the man who loves his brother wants to keep living in the light.

The other mark of a true Christian, according to John, is that 'There is none occasion of stumbling in him' (v. 10). That is to say, the true Christian walks so as to give no intentional offence. He does not make others stumble, for the Word of Jesus is being fulfilled in his life. Lack of love does untold harm in any Christian fellowship, and also prevents people in this dark world from coming to hear the Word of God.

Are you living in such a way that no one will be able to say, 'You prevented me from coming to Christ'? Do you lead others to the Lamb of God who takes away the sin of the world?

The second person that John presents is the professing Christian who fails the test of love. John says, 'He that hateth his brother is in darkness, and walketh in darkness, and knoweth not whither he goeth, because that darkness hath blinded his eyes' (v. 11).

John tells us three things about the false professor. First, he is 'in darkness, even unto now' (v. 9). He has not been transferred from the realm of darkness into the kingdom of light. It does not matter what the professor claims to be or to know; he may claim, like the Gnostics, to have much light and to know many things, but if his actions show that he hates his brother, he lives in the realm of darkness.

Second, the false professor walks in darkness (v. 11). The person who does not love his brother is living according to the dictates of his sinful nature. He cannot walk in the light because he does not have a new nature that enables him to walk in the light. That is evident in how he lives.

Third, such a person is blind. He cannot see and does not know where he is going because darkness has covered his eyes. No matter how much light comes his way, the darkness in his heart so blinds his soul that he can only stumble about.

The Pharisees of Jesus' day were false professors. When Jesus told them they were blind leaders of the blind, they were indignant. 'What are you saying? Are we blind also?' Jesus said they were blind because they did not know the truth. They claimed to know what a relationship with God was all about, but the way they lived proved that they were not walking in the light. They were blind to the truth of Jesus Christ, God's Son. Because of that, they would stumble down the road of darkness all the way to hell.

Failing to love is a serious matter. People get angry at other people. In time, resentment and bitterness takes over their hearts. It does not matter what they profess to believe; what shows is what is uppermost in their minds. When they go to work, bitterness lies heavy on their souls. When they go to bed at night, anger surfaces again. The darkness is always there, blinding them to everything else. That is what John is telling us here. If you do not love your brother and sister in Christ, you are walking in darkness, and the darkness is so blinding your eyes that you cannot see the light of Jesus.

## Testing Ourselves by This Command

We are either in darkness or in light. If we are unwilling to love others, we are in darkness, but if the gospel has broken into our hearts, it so rearranges our souls and reshapes our priorities that we cannot help but love Christ and others. That love is evidence that we live in the light.

We can test ourselves by the commandment of love by asking the following questions: Do we love our family members? Do we habitually show kindness every day to everyone in our family? Do we think loving thoughts about them, speak loving words, and do loving acts? Obedience to God's commandment to love begins at home.

Do we love our brothers and sisters in the church, or do we just tolerate them? God commands us to love especially the household of faith (Gal. 6:10). Do we love some believers but not others? If we say we love them, do our prayers reveal that? Is our heart knit with theirs, not just by words but by our actions and attitudes? Do we weep with those that weep and rejoice with those that rejoice?

Do we love our extended human family — our neighbours, classmates, work associates, bosses? Are we treating them like the Samaritan treated his hurting neighbour? John teaches us that we must not talk about how we love God and walk in the light if we ignore our neighbour when he or she is in need. If we do not show love to our neighbour, we walk in darkness that blinds us and will lead us to hell if we do not repent and turn to God.

Finally, remember two things. First, let us remember that brotherly love is a command, not an option. Love, ultimately, is not a matter of feeling; it is a matter of obedience. It is an attitude that works itself out practically in loving words and actions.

Love takes effort, resolve, faith, and grace. But above all, it requires a deep awareness of God's amazing love for you. You will never make strides forward in brotherly love until you are struck by the wonder of God's love to you. That will be the great impulse for you to love other believers with all kinds of personality flaws. When you are overwhelmed by God's love for you, a hell-deserving sinner, then your heart will flow out to others quite readily, even to those whose personalities are not lovable. Your love for them will assure you and others that you are a child of God (1 John 3:14).

Second, brotherly love is not perfect in this life. Every child of God feels that he falls short in loving others. John felt that, too. The darkness is passing away, John says in verse 8, but it has not yet fully passed away. The light has come but not yet in its full splendour. Robert Candlish writes in his commentary: 'We need to ask ourselves this question: Is the darkness a lingering friend to me or a departing stranger?'

All of this means there are still temptations and hidden snares in the believer's life. The world is full of temptations, John says, but brotherly love will guard you from succumbing to them. You would think he would say that loving the Father or loving Christ will keep you from giving in to temptation. That is true, but John's point is that loving the people of God will keep you from falling into sin because God loves to guard those who love his children.

Here, then, is one more evidence of being in the light, of being a true Christian. The church is not merely a group of individuals meeting together to worship. The church is the family of God. Are you part of that family? Does your life show that you are part of that family?

# 8

## The Test of Experience

*I write unto you, little children, because your sins are forgiven you for his name's sake. I write unto you, fathers, because ye have known him that is from the beginning. I write unto you, young men, because ye have overcome the wicked one. I write unto you, little children, because ye have known the Father. I have written unto you, fathers, because ye have known him that is from the beginning. I have written unto you, young men, because ye are strong, and the word of God abideth in you, and ye have overcome the wicked one (1 John 2:12–14).*

In 1 John 2, John offers five tests for self-examination: the test of obedience (vv. 3–6), the test of love (vv. 7–11), the test of experience (vv. 12–14), the test of worldliness (vv. 15–17), and the test of doctrinal soundness (vv. 18–29). The test of experience is unique in this list. That is because in verses 12–14, John pauses to present us with some important teaching about what should be true of all Christians before continuing with his call to self-examination.

## Why John Pauses

John pauses, first, to remind his readers how serious he is about the urgency of his topic. Notice the intensely personal nature of his writing. He says, 'I write' three times as he addresses 'little children', 'young men', and 'fathers'. John was deeply concerned about the spiritual welfare of those to whom he was writing, particularly because of the heresy that was creeping into the church and threatening the spiritual well-being of believers.

Second, John pauses to remind his readers of the foundations of their faith. He realizes that much of his teaching has been intensely soul-searching and can be disturbing, even for true believers. Satan might twist John's words to dishearten many of the weaker believers; some of the 'little children' might even question how they could hope to meet the standards John upheld for true faith. John pauses here to remind believers of their experiential foundations in Christ, and of what God did for them in bringing them to saving faith. He encourages believers by reminding them of what they possess in Christ, so they will have the heart to press forward in obedience to the Word of God, to love others, and to separate themselves from the world.

## John's Readers

John makes six statements about his readers in verses 12–14, arranged in two sets of three statements each. In each set, the first statement is addressed to 'little children', the second to 'fathers', and the third to 'young men'. Commentaries differ about the categories of people that John addresses in these verses. Some commentators say that John offers three ways of looking at all Christians, thus each statement applies to all believers. That approach does not seem to fit the context or content of what John is saying, even though every believer needs to hear and apply all of John's statements.

Commentators such as Luther and Calvin think that John is referring here to only two categories of people: fathers and young men, or the mature and the immature. They view the term *little children* as applicable to all believers. They cite 1 John 2:1, in which John says, 'My little children, these things write I unto you', saying that John is addressing the entire family of God, referring to them in an affectionate way as his little children. But is he using that term here, or is he speaking of another category distinct from fathers and young men? Furthermore, why does John use a different word for little children in verse 13 (*paidia*, i.e., school-age children) than the one that he uses in verse 12 (*teknia*, i.e., offspring)? Is he referring to literal age groups in the church? Or is he referring to levels of spiritual maturity usually evident in various groups in the church?

Given the parallelism that John uses here by referring to each group twice, I believe that he does have three groups in mind. It is difficult to come to any other conclusion when you compare verse 12 with verse 13c, verse 13a with verse 14a, and verse 13b with verse 14b. Though the general context of the epistle indicates that 'little children' in verse 12 (*teknia*) usually refers to the entire church, since John uses it several times that way in his first epistle (2:1, 18, 28; 3:7, 18; 4:4; 5:21), the immediate context of our verses justifies three levels of experience. Moreover, the second word translated in verse 13 as 'little children' is *paidia*, which definitely means young children.

It is unlikely that John is simply writing to different age groups here, because we all know Christians who are ripe in age but young in grace, and others who are young in age but ripe in grace. Even if there was a growing tendency in John's third Christian generation for spiritual maturity and natural age to coincide, John is still emphasizing spiritual experience. God's family, like *every* human family, contains members of different maturity.

We conclude that the strict parallelism of verses 12 through 14 indicates that the safest way to interpret these verses, as Augustine has said, is to see John speaking to three groups in various stages of spiritual development. It is as if John says, 'I write unto you who have recently come to faith and are but children in grace, I write unto you fathers who for many years have walked with the Saviour and have proved the faithfulness of God, and I write unto you young men who are growing in grace and must labour in Christ as you wrestle for mastery over sin and Satan.'

The repetition of the three groups and the messages addressed to each is John's way of emphasizing the privileges they possess in Christ. It is also John's way of making clear his warm affection for believers and his deep concern for their spiritual welfare. But the most important thing to notice is that John, in each of these cases, is dealing with foundational Christian experience according to the different stages of true believers' Christian lives. The young convert, whom John calls 'little child', is a recent convert. He is newly aware that his sins have been forgiven, and he is beginning to appreciate what it means to have God as his Father. So John says in verse 12, 'I write unto you, little children, because your sins are forgiven you for his name's sake' and in verse 13, 'I write unto you, little children, because ye have known the Father.'

What a joy it is in those first days after conversion to cling to Christ the Saviour and God as Father, to learn about God, to delight in him, to depend on him, to be embraced by him, to sing his name in praises and petitions before the throne of grace! The joy of forgiveness and a personal relationship with God are most precious to young converts.

Although the new believer has experienced the goodness of the Father and wants to behave like an obedient child, he has little experience in doing so. He has much love for God and a tender conscience for God, but he does not understand the warfare of daily sanctification, the intense battles of daily Christian living, or the need to live out of Christ continually. His simplicity and strength of faith as well as the brightness and joy of his initial experiences of grace and forgiveness are a gracious blessing for the church, yet he has so much to learn. He depends too much on his feelings at a given moment; he is lifted high in times of obedience and fresh communion with God, then plunges low in times of disobedience or feeling apart from the Father. He is both easily encouraged and easily discouraged. He knows little about what is expected of him, but he is hungry and thirsty to know more.

Fathers in the faith are spiritually mature and stable. They have come to know the eternal God in Christ in an intimate way. John stresses the fathers' consciousness of the immutable, eternal God of grace by saying twice in verses 13 and 14 that he writes to fathers 'because ye have known him that is from the beginning'.

Fathers focus on Christ. They have insights into the wonders of Christ's glorious person and his distinctive offices. They see him as the centre of all Jehovah's counsels, the image of the invisible God, and the One in whom all the promises of God are fulfilled (Eph. 3:11; 2 Cor. 1:21).

The experience of fathers in Christ is more complete than that of young men in Christ. Like Mnason, who Acts 21:16 says was 'an old disciple', these fathers are old, experienced disciples in a spiritual sense. Their knowledge is deeply rooted (Col. 1:23), influential, and stable (Phil. 1:9; Eph. 3:18). They are settled in the truth, prudent, sober, and self-controlled (Eph. 4:14; Tit. 2:2). Faith and obedience are evident in their lives. They have a mature understanding of the ways of holiness and are equipped to practise holiness in the strength of Christ. They have experienced that the Lord Jesus Christ is an excellent master to serve. They have experienced how patiently God has borne with their ignorance, how graciously he has pardoned their sins, and how faithfully he has supplied their needs. Christ's goodness moves them to exercise love, obedience, and gratitude. They have reached, in some measure, what Paul calls 'the stature of the fulness of Christ' (Eph. 4:13).

The Word of God dwells richly in spiritual fathers. Their good spiritual sense, experiential life in Christ, and seasoned counsel benefit the church of God. Paul said, 'For though ye have ten thousand instructors in Christ, yet have ye not many fathers' (2 Cor. 4:15). Fathers guide the ignorant as well as the children and young men in the faith. Their winsome lives move others to emulate their Christ-centredness. Their conversation is rich with talk of Christ. They know how to speak to children and young men, to the broken-hearted and the doubting. They can discern between form and power, hypocrisy and sincerity.

They know how to resist foolish ideas and enterprises that will not prosper the church. They have a great responsibility to help a congregation focus on the triune God and his truth, and to maintain the purity of the gospel.

Between the new converts and the mature Christians are the young men in the faith. A young man in his twenties is partly mature and partly immature, but he is gaining experience from the rigours of daily adult life. Similarly, these spiritual young men are being prepared for full Christian duty in the thick of the battle and in bearing the burden and heat of everyday troubles. They represent the church's first line of defence against attack in the midst of the strain of Christian living. They search the Scriptures with spiritual vigour, are fervent in faith, mighty in prayer, intense in action, and bold in testimony. They are strong in Christ, endure by Christ, and resist attack through Christ.

These converted young men are grateful that God has broken the reign of sin and Satan in their lives. Though they still stumble and fall into error, just as young men are apt to do in life, they have felt the thrill of spiritual victory. They have been made strong by grace through the Word; they earnestly contend for the faith and are often able to overcome the wicked one. Their conflicts often become conquests.

Yet these young men lack maturity. Their experience is by no means complete. They struggle hard against ungodliness, but they need to persevere in grace. They have yet to learn that 'old Satan may prove too much for young Melanchthon'. They often think too much of themselves and are affected by emotional highs and lows. Too often they are more impressed by what they have been doing and how they feel than by what God has been doing and how God feels. They need to live more for the glory of God, not themselves.

These are the three types of people is addressing. The little children are the young converts, the fathers are mature Christians, and the young men are growing toward maturity through daily battles with sin and Satan. All three groups are a blessing to the church: the children are the church's reaching hand; the young men, the church's strong arm; the mature fathers, the church's backbone. Children represent the church's tender love, young men the church's strength, fathers the church's knowledge. Yet each group of believers has its weaknesses. Children in the faith are prone to make too much of what they feel, young men make too much of what they do, and fathers make too much of what they know. As John says, believers in all three categories need the constant, daily ministry of the Holy Spirit to remain unspotted from the world.

**Three Foundations of Faith**

John wants Christians of all levels of maturity to reflect upon something that applies to all Christians. He mentions three foundational truths in the first three sentences and repeats then with some variation in the second three sentences. John wants to emphasize the foundations upon which believers' lives have been built so that they might be encouraged to go forward and build upon these foundations:

1. *Their sins are forgiven.* John says in verse 12, 'I write unto you, little children, because your sins are forgiven you for his name's sake.' When the Holy Spirit begins to work in the life of sinners, the first thing they become conscious of is their sin. When Jesus was teaching the disciples in the upper room, he told them, 'When the Holy Spirit is come unto you, he will convince the world of sin, and of righteousness, and of judgement' (John 16:7).

    One of the first and greatest promises in the gospel of our Lord Jesus Christ is that we can find forgiveness of sins. When Peter's listeners became convicted of their sin as he preached on the day of Pentecost, they cried out, 'Men and brethren, what shall we do?' Peter told them, 'Repent, and be baptized every one of you in the name of Jesus Christ for the remission of sins' (Acts 2:38–39).

    John thus writes to children in faith to assure them that their sins are forgiven only for Christ's sake. He tells them, in effect, 'Be encouraged that you have been forgiven and adopted into the family of God. Do not take these privileges for granted. Never lose sight of them. Remember that your justification is perfect; it cannot be lost nor improved upon.'

The false teachers of John's day were forcing new believers to doubt their salvation. John assures them, 'I will tell you why I am writing to you: because your sins have been forgiven.' Assurance of the forgiveness of sin is a major need of all believers. What a privilege, an unspeakable joy, and a powerful blessing forgiveness is!

2.  *They know the Father and the Son.* John says in verse 13, 'I write unto you, fathers, because ye have known him that is from the beginning.' Later, he says, 'I write unto you, little children, because ye have known the Father.'

    When we know our sins are forgiven by God, we learn to know God as our Father. When the prodigal came home in repentance, his father ran to meet his son, fell upon his neck, and kissed him. The sins of the boy were blotted out, and he was received back again into the family. Similarly, when forgives our sins, he adopts us into his family and we come to know him as our Father.

    The Gnostics were telling believers they did not know God because they lacked the special knowledge and experience that the Gnostics had. John says, 'I am writing to you because you have known the Father. God is your Father. You have come to know him. You are his child. Nothing will *ever* change that.'

    In deciding whether or not you are a true Christian who knows God, ask yourself, how do I pray? Do not consider so much *what* you pray as *how* you pray. Do you pray as a son or daughter to a loving Father who gave his only Son for you, or do you pray as a stranger? When my children come to me, they do not ask, 'Sir, could we have an appointment?' They say, 'Dad, can I talk to you?' They address me as a father because they have a relationship with me. They can be intimate with me in a way that no one else can.

When the child of God prays, a sense of the fatherliness of God, fostered by the Spirit, encourages him to call God 'Father'. Jesus said that when we pray we should say, 'Our Father'. The Spirit inspires us with the confidence to call the God of heaven 'Father' (Rom. 8:15).

The one who has made this relationship with the Father possible is the eternal Son of God, whom John refers to as the one who was in and from the beginning (1:1, 2). As we mature in faith, we come to appreciate the eternal nature of the Father's love toward us in Christ. We marvel at what God said in Jeremiah 31:3: 'Yea, I have loved thee with an everlasting love: therefore with loving kindness have I drawn thee.'

3. *They have victory over sin and Satan.* Notice how John uses the past tense when he says, 'I have written unto you, young men, because ye are strong, and the word of God abideth in you, and ye have overcome the wicked one' (v. 14).

Some churches teach that we need a second blessing of the Holy Spirit to have victory over sin. The apostles do not teach that. Paul says in Romans 6 that a Christian has died to sin and no longer lives under its dominion. That is exactly what John teaches here. He says that when a person becomes a Christian, the reign of sin is broken; the Spirit of life in Christ Jesus has made us free from the law of sin and death. That does not mean that the Christian will have no more battles with sin, no more failures, no more weakness, and no more defeat. It means that he has come into a realm in which sin and Satan have been defeated through the work of the cross. He has been introduced by the indwelling Spirit to a power that enables him to live for God in this world.

John says this victory over sin continues. In verse 14 he says, 'Ye are strong ... and ye have overcome the wicked one.' Believers have the ongoing strength to overcome sin and Satan because the Word of God dwells in them. That echoes what the psalmist said in Psalm 119: 'Wherewithal shall a young man cleanse his way? by taking heed thereto according to thy word ... Thy word have I hid in mine heart, that I might not sin against thee' (vv. 9, 11).

If we are to have victory in the midst of a hostile world dominated by sin and Satan, we must remember that when God saved us and gave new life, he gave us power to live in this world as we ought to live. He gave us power to overcome sin and Satan and to live victoriously for the glory of God.

Though the world will do anything to divert young believers from Christ, John encourages and challenges them by reminding them that they are children of God, but also soldiers for Christ: 'I write to you because ye have overcome the wicked one ... I write to you because ye are strong, and the word of God abideth in you.' In other words, they have overcome the evil one and will continue to overcome him. They are in the front lines of battle, though, because the Christian life is at war with the world, the flesh, and the devil.

The Christian enjoys the privileges of God's love and forgiveness, but he is also called to engage in the fight of faith. God offers us every encouragement in this fight. Remember, the cause is good; it is a *good* fight of faith. Remember, too, that the battle is the Lord's. We fight under the leadership of Jesus Christ, who has never turned back and has never failed us. He has conquered our greatest enemies and those of many of your brothers and sisters in faith have preceded you.

The devil is a real enemy, not an imaginary foe. John writes, 'I have written unto you, young men, because ye are strong, and the word of God abideth in you and ye have overcome the wicked one.' Notice the connection here between having the Word of God in one's heart and overcoming the evil one. Perhaps John was thinking here about Jesus' temptation in the wilderness. At the beginning of our Lord's public ministry, Satan came to tempt Jesus in the wilderness, offering him the kingdoms of the world in three different ways. Jesus responded to each temptation by quoting from Scripture: 'It is written', he said three times, quoting from Deuteronomy. Jesus had so hidden God's Word in his heart that when temptation came, he had the resources of his Father to beat back the enemy.

By grace, believers also overcome evil through the living Word of God, Jesus Christ. John encourages us by showing us that no matter where we are in our spiritual pilgrimage, the Word of God helps us see through the wiles of the devil.

Be thankful for what God has granted you, and strive to grow in grace. Make the best use of what you read, hear, and see. Aim to be a father in faith, and pray for grace to live like one.

Fathers, lay aside childish things. Young men, be strong in Christ Jesus. Children, obey your Father who is in heaven. And every one of you, remember that God builds us up by the same means with which he saved us — his Word and his Spirit. Search the Word, depend on the Spirit, and look to Christ.

# 9

## The Test of Worldliness

*Love not the world, neither the things that are in the world. If any man love the world, the love of the Father is not in him. For all that is in the world, the lust of the flesh, and the lust of the eyes, and the pride of life, is not of the Father, but is of the world. And the world passeth away, and the lust thereof: but he that doeth the will of God abideth for ever* (1 John 2:15-17).

In this passage, the Apostle John contrasts love for the world with love for the Father. These two loves are incompatible. Either you love God or you love the world; you cannot love both. Jesus said, 'No man can serve two masters: for either he will hate the one, and love the other; or else he will hold to the one, and despise the other' (Matt. 6:24).

One love must rule our life: one holy passion for God and the things of God. The choice is clear and the directions simple, but the way is not easy. The appeal of the world is strong, and the flesh is weak.

### The Essence of Worldliness

John offers two important reasons why we should not love the world. First, the world is opposed to God. *Kosmos*, or 'world', has several meanings in the New Testament. In 1 John 2:15-17, the apostle is not referring to the physical world in which we live nor the mass of people living on the planet. Rather, he uses the term to refer to a kingdom, its ruler and its inhabitants, lost in sin and wholly at odds with anything divine or pleasing to God. He is talking about Satan's kingdom of darkness that includes all people who are under his dominion. 'World' here has an ethical, spiritual connotation, set in contrast to Christ and his church. This world does not know God or his Son but crucified the Lord of glory (John 1:10). It refers to 'this present evil world' (John 8:23) as opposed to the other world, the heavenly world.

This world, though created to reflect the glory of God, now exists in rebellion against the Lord and against his Christ (Ps. 2:2). It has become a fallen, disordered world lying in the grip of the evil one (1 John 5:19). Despite its great achievements, this world is lost. It is incapable of saving itself. It has lost its purpose. It can no longer glorify God. The world is the mass of mankind estranged from God through sin, living after the lusts of the flesh.

Worldliness, then, is human activity without God. Someone who is of this world is controlled by what preoccupies the world: the quest for pleasure, profit, and position. He yields to the spirit of fallen mankind: the spirit of self-seeking, self-indulgence without regard for God. Each one of us, by nature, was born like this. We are attached to the world. We are in tune with the spirit of the world. We belong to this evil world; it is our natural habitat.

We are dead in trespasses and sins and are children of wrath (Eph. 2:1-2) until God graciously regenerates us and makes us his own (John 3:5). Only then are we set apart from fallen mankind and called out of this sinful world to become living members of the church and kingdom of God. Regeneration, or the new birth, divides the world into the kingdom of God and the realm of Satan, which war against each other.

As Christians we are still attracted to the world because of the sin that remains in us. The sinful flesh in us is inclined toward the world. That is why isolation from the world cannot keep us from sin. We carry a piece of the world within us wherever we go.

With the world, the devil, and the flesh against us, is there any hope for victory? Absolutely, for that victory was won when Jesus defeated Satan on the cross and rose from the dead. In John 15:19, Jesus said, 'Ye are not of the world, but I have chosen you out of the world.' God's people have been plucked from the kingdom of this world and now belong to Christ and the kingdom of heaven. In Christ, by the Spirit's grace, we overcome the world, but we must also fight daily against the temptations of the world. John names three ways in which we are lured back into the ways of the world: the lust of the flesh, the lust of the eyes, and the pride of life.

## The Paths of Worldliness

Verse 16 tells us, 'For all that is in the world, the lust of the flesh, and the lust of the eyes, and the pride of life, is not of the Father, but is of the world.' These lusts deal ultimately with heart sins, with our inner core nature. Yet these internal enemies are often aroused and fed by external temptations. We must therefore be specific as we warn one another about separating ourselves and our children from these paths of worldliness named by John.

First, we must beware of *the lust of the flesh*. Lust refers to that which the flesh desires. We must not love a world that delights in the lusts of the flesh. That means resisting many temptations, such as substance abuse — whether in the form of drugs, smoking, overeating, or excessive drinking of alcohol — as well as all forms sexual immorality, including things that provoke it such as flirtation and immodesty. Refusing to love the world means keeping ourselves and our children from anything that incites the lusts of the flesh. We must not be brought under bondage to anything physical but are to be self-controlled, for our body is the temple of the Holy Ghost (1 Cor. 3:17; 6:12; 9:27). We are called to freedom as God's children (Rom. 8).

If you are in doubt about whether you should become involved in something, ask yourself: Can I pray over this? Does it glorify God or ignite fleshly lusts? Does it pass the test of Philippians 4:8, being honest, just, pure, lovely, and of good report? If it encourages lust, rid yourself of it as much as you can. Do not love this present evil world, but 'put ye on the Lord Jesus Christ, and make not provision for the flesh, to fulfil the lusts thereof' (Rom. 13:14).

Second, John warns against the *lust of the eyes* — i.e., that which our natural, sinful eyes desire. Say no to all forms of entertainment that pander to the lust of the eyes by glamourizing sin. Such forms of entertainment make adultery and fornication look innocent, commonplace, or else exciting. Murder becomes thrilling. Profanity is acceptable everyday speech.

Let us rid our homes of unedifying magazines, trashy novels, and profane books — indeed, all printed and visual material that contradicts the Ten Commandments. How can we pray not to be led into temptation while we continue to play with the fire of temptation? As James warns us, 'Every man is tempted, when he is drawn away of his own lust, and enticed. Then when lust hath conceived, it bringeth forth sin: and sin, when it is finished, bringeth forth death' (James 1:14-15).

Turn your eyes from whatever seems to incite the lust of the eyes. Practise self-denial. Like Job, make a covenant with your eyes to set no wicked thing before you (Job 31:1).

Finally, John warns against *the pride of life*. That refers to vain glory, to displaying ourselves in how we live. How prevalent such pride is in our hearts. George Swinnock said, 'Pride is the first shirt we put on in Paradise and the last we will take off when we die.' The pride of life includes being proud of ourselves, our accomplishments, our possessions, and even our religion. It can involve idolizing ourselves or others, including movie actors, sports heroes, government leaders, or other popular figures.

Such pride is at the root of our hearts. By nature we are filled with self-gratification, self-contentment, and self-fulfilment. We want to rule our own destiny. We live for ourselves, applauding our own wisdom and accomplishments.

Do we engage in holy warfare against all three of these paths? Do we walk different from the world? Are we pilgrims and strangers on the earth? My people 'shall dwell alone, and shall not be reckoned among the nations', God says in Numbers 23:9. Can that be said of us? Do we love the Father, or do we love the world? Eternal consequences hinge upon our answers to these questions.

## The Curse of Worldliness

God curses worldliness, John says, for 'the world passeth away, and the lust thereof (v. 17). That's the second reason John cites for not loving the world. The world's best pleasures are temporary. The world is our passage, not our portion. Our death dates are on God's calendar. As Hebrews 9:27 says, 'It is appointed unto men once to die, but after this the judgement.'

The world will one day be burned up, along with all of those who lust after the world's sinful pleasures. So if you live your life according to the lust of the flesh, the lust of the eye, and the pride of life, what have you acquired? Charles Spurgeon said, 'If you got all the world, you would have got nothing after your coffin lid was screwed down but gravedust in your mouth.'

The world never gives what it promises. It is a mirage, a fraud, a hollow bubble. John Trapp wrote, 'Pleasure, profit, and preferment are the worldling's trinity.' Long ago, Solomon discovered all three to be vanity. When you read Ecclesiastes, you will understand why John Bunyan called the world Vanity Fair.

## Deliverance from Worldliness

Deliverance from worldliness is possible only by doing the will of God, John tells us (v. 17c). But what does that involve?

• We must realize that it is crucial to *fight against worldliness*. If we are not convinced of that, we will make little progress in spiritual life. James 1:27 tells us 'Pure religion and undefiled before God and the Father is this, To visit the fatherless and widows in their affliction, and to keep himself unspotted from the world.' The purity of our walk with God is directly related to our commitment not to allow the world to stain the garments of righteousness that God has given us.

• We must use every means to *conquer worldliness*. Every day we should examine ourselves, repent before God, mortify our flesh, walk in the Spirit, and put on the whole armour of God (Eph. 6:10-20). We should listen to sermons, saturate ourselves with Scripture, meditate on the Word, read books that can make us wise to salvation, and pray without ceasing. We should fellowship with believers, observe the Lord's Day, evangelize unbelievers, and serve others.

• We must *trust our great High Priest and his Spirit*. When the power of the world threatens to invade our souls, we can take comfort in remembering that our great High Priest prayed, 'Father, I pray not that thou shouldest take them out of the world [here "world" is used in the sense of this earth], but that thou shouldest keep them from the evil' (John 17:15). When every defence seems down and we are most vulnerable to yielding to the enemy of our souls, we may yet hope for deliverance through the intercession of Jesus Christ and the preserving power of his Spirit. We may cry out, 'Were it not for the Saviour's intercession and the Spirit's preservation, we would have been swept into evil in the hour of temptation.'

Spurgeon wrote, 'I thank God that when temptation is present, he removes my desire, and when desire to sin is present, he removes the temptation.' This is the gracious gift of Jesus Christ who promises that he will pray for us in the hour of temptation that our faith will not fail (Luke 22:32).

• We must *meditate more on our future*. Remember that the world and its lusts pass away, 'but he that doeth the will of God abideth for ever' (v. 17). If we are believers, full deliverance will be ours in the never-ending age to come. Right now, heaven is in our hearts and in our deepest affections, yet the world and the devil are still at our elbow. But in the age to come, nothing but righteousness will dwell in the new heavens and the new earth. The world that is under the curse of God and the prince of the power of the air will be no more. Satan and all of his followers will be banished to eternal perdition, and the people of God will shine in the firmament of God's glory.

# 10

# The Test of Sound Doctrine

*Little children, it is the last time: and as ye have heard that antichrist shall come, even now are there many antichrists; whereby we know that it is the last time. They went out from us, but they were not of us; for if they had been of us, they would no doubt have continued with us: but they went out, that they might be made manifest that they were not all of us. But ye have an unction from the Holy One, and ye know all things. I have not written unto you because ye know not the truth, but because ye know it, and that no lie is of the truth. Who is a liar but he that denieth that Jesus is the Christ? He is antichrist, that denieth the Father and the Son. Whosoever denieth the Son, the same hath not the Father: but he that acknowledgeth the Son hath the Father also. Let that therefore abide in you, which ye have heard from the beginning. If that which ye have heard from the beginning shall remain in you, ye also shall continue in the Son, and in the Father. And this is the promise that he hath promised us, even eternal life. These things have I written unto you concerning them that seduce you. But the anointing which ye have received of him abideth in you, and ye need not that any man teach you: but as the same anointing teacheth you of all things, and is truth, and is no lie, and even as it hath taught you, ye shall abide in him* (1 John 2:18-27).

Until now John has been focusing on how Christians behave. Gnostic teachers were telling believers in the church that it did not matter what a person did; what mattered was having certain experiences of God and being introduced to mysteries through divine enlightenment. John countered that teaching by saying that if we claim to have fellowship with Christ, yet live heedless of his commandments, we deceive ourselves. John then goes on to answer the critical question: What shapes and directs the daily lives of God's people?

In the first part of chapter 2, John says our lives must be shaped by God's commandments (vv. 3–6), brotherly love (vv. 7–11), Christian experience (vv. 12–14), and separation from the ungodly world (vv. 15–17). John has told us that we must pattern our lives according to what God has spoken, not according to the attitudes and opinions of the world.

In verse 18, John turns from how Christians behave to what Christians believe, setting before us in ten verses the test of sound doctrine. Let us look at three aspects of sound doctrine: the importance of sound doctrine in 'the last hour', how antichrists fail to maintain sound doctrine, and the cultivation of sound doctrine by Spirit-anointed faith.

## The Last Hour

'Little children, it is the last time: and as ye have heard that antichrist shall come, even now are there many antichrists; whereby we know that it is the last time' (v. 18). John is speaking more in terms of theology than chronology. He does not mean that within a few days Christ will return from glory and bring history to an end. The last time (literally, John says in Greek, 'the last hour') in the New Testament is the whole span of time, however long or short, between Jesus' return to heaven and his second coming to earth. We, like John's first readers, are living 'in the last hour'.

John talks of this time as the last hour because God has only one appointment on his calendar he has yet to keep. Imagine God having a calendar throughout the ages, marking off one great event after another as it comes to pass. The one event remaining on that calendar is the return of the Lord Jesus Christ to this earth in power and glory.

After he had prophesied his own return at the last day, Jesus warned his disciples, 'Therefore be ye also ready: for in such an hour as ye think not the Son of man cometh' (Matt. 24:44). We do not know the day or the hour when Christ will return; it may be generations from now, or it may be today. None of us may live to see Christ's return, but we all need to ask ourselves: Do I really believe this is the last hour? Am I prepared to appear before Christ's judgement seat (2 Cor. 5:10)? Have I been born again, convicted of my sin and unrighteousness, drawn to faith in Christ's righteousness, and brought to live before God in holiness and gratitude?

## The Antichrists

One sign that convinced John that the last time had come was the activity of people who he calls 'antichrists'. Verse 18 says, 'Even now are there many antichrists; whereby we know that it is the last time.'

Today many people are fascinated with the idea of the Antichrist. The word *antichrist* means 'the opposite of Christ' or 'instead of Christ'. So the Antichrist is either the utter opposite of Christ because of his wickedness and his efforts to thwart salvation, or he is someone who claims to stand in the place of Christ as the Saviour of the world. He may be both. John is the only New Testament writer who uses the term *antichrist,* though Daniel 7–11, 2 Thessalonians 2, 1 Timothy 4, 2 Peter 2–3, and Revelation 13 all address this topic.

Jesus himself warned his disciples about false christs and false prophets. Jesus said that in the last day people would claim to be Christ, the last prophet, or the final revelation of God. Jesus said that we should have nothing to do with such people, because when he comes again, the whole cosmos will know it.

Who are these antichrists? John is very specific. He says the Antichrist will one day come, but right now, many antichrists are among us. These antichrists are forerunners of the ultimate

Antichrist who will stridently oppose Christ in the world. They
are possessed by the evil one and are enemies of God, but they
are ordinary men and women — not devils or demons. They
do not wear badges that say, 'I am an antichrist.' No doubt you
could pass antichrists in the street or sit next to them in church
and not recognize them as such. But we do know some things
about these people who are against Christ, his church, his kingdom, his gospel, and his people.

**Antichrists in the Church**

First, John says, antichrists were once in the church: 'Whereby
we know that it is the last time, [for] they went out from us' (v.
19). For a time, antichrists profess to be Christians. But in time
they leave the visible fellowship of the people of God.

They leave the church, John says, because 'they were not
of us' (v. 19). They were in the midst of the church and partici-
pated in its affairs, but they did not really belong to the people of God, 'for if they had been of us, they would no doubt
have continued with us' (v.19). In other words, these people
who leave the church and are now living apart from Christ were
never converted. They were not born of the Spirit of God.

John implies two reasons why they went out. First, they
could no longer bear to listen to God's Word. God's Word so
oppressed their conscience that they wanted to be free of that
burden. Second, they were unwilling to pay the cost of being a
Christian. In John's day, being a Christian meant you might lose
everything. You might be cast out of the family home and dis-
inherited. You might be laughed at and scorned by the world.
These people who left the church were no longer willing to suffer the consequences of being faithful, confession Christ before
men.

True Christians may temporarily fall away, but they do not
do so permanently and become antichrists. We should ask ourselves, 'Am I in danger of drifting?' That is how falling away
usually begins. It begins quietly in the heart, with a disaffected
spirit. Slowly that spirit alienates you from others. You become
like a ship without any mooring that slowly drifts away from

harbour and disappears from sight. We must heed the Lord's words, 'He that shall endure unto the end, the same shall be saved' (Matt. 24:13).

John also tells us that not everyone in the church is truly of the church. Being part of the Christian community is not synonymous with being united to Jesus Christ. Church members may share the earthly company of God's people but not their heavenly birth. At present, the visible church is a mixed multitude. Only the last day will reveal who truly was in Christ and who was merely in the church. The real issue for us is not, am I a faithful church attender, but, do I belong to Christ? Am I joined to him by a true faith?

## Antichrists and Christ

The second characteristic of antichrists, John says (vv. 22–23), is that they deny that Jesus is the Messiah. 'Who is a liar but he that denieth that Jesus is the Christ? He is antichrist, that denieth the Father and the Son' (v. 22).

The word *Christ* is the Greek equivalent of the Hebrew word, *Messiah*. Both words mean 'the Anointed One'. In the Old Testament, prophets were anointed by God to speak God's word to his people. Priests were anointed to offer sacrifices for sin and to intercede for God's people. Kings were anointed to rule over God's people. Jesus came as the Christ, the anointed prophet, priest, and king of God's people. John says the antichrists deny that Jesus is the Christ, God's last word as prophet, God's only sacrifice for sin as priest, and God's appointed King to rule forever.

The Gnostics separated the divine Christ from the human Jesus. They taught that the divine Christ came down upon the human Jesus, but then left him at the cross. They posited two persons, where John sees only one: 'Jesus' *is* 'the Christ'. From the very first, Jesus was announced as the Christ: 'For unto you is born this day in the city of David a Saviour, which is Christ the Lord' (Luke 2:11).

The antichrists who deny that Jesus is the Christ are also without the Father. John boldly declares in verse 23, 'Whosoever denieth the Son, the same hath not the Father'. He reminds us that what we believe about Jesus determines where we will spend eternity.

## Cultivating Sound Doctrine

Antichristian teaching and antichrists are everywhere, always trying to lead Christians astray, John says (v. 26). They want us to wander away from Christ. They want to seduce us and to deceive us. How can we guard ourselves against being taken in by false teaching and becoming antichrists?

John gives us two antidotes to false teaching, or two ways to pass the test of soundness in the faith. First, we must direct our lives according to the Word of God. Verse 24 says, 'Let that therefore abide in you, which ye have heard from the beginning.' To stay on course and not be blown in every direction, to press on while avoiding the dangerous rocks that would smash our faith, we must keep on believing the Word of God. Let it remain in you, John says. Be like the psalmist, who said, 'Thy word have I hid in mine heart, that I might not sin against thee' (Ps. 119:11).

We ought to read the Scriptures daily to inform our minds and nourish our souls so that when temptations come, whether moral or theological, our hearts will be taken up with Christ and his truth and we will say, 'How can I believe or do what is against Christ? How can I sin against God who has loved me, who gave his Son for me, and who is preparing a home in heaven for me?'

Many people pay lip service to the Word; they may admire it, but they do not feed upon it. When we neglect to read God's Word daily, we slip loose from our anchor. When we read and digest God's Word, it is imprinted on our souls and our defences are reinforced against false teaching. So we must anchor our minds and hearts in God's Word and Bible-based literature.

The second antidote to false teaching is to heed the ministry of God's Spirit. In verses 20 and 27, John says of believers: 'But ye have an unction from the Holy One, and ye know all things. But the anointing which ye have received of him abideth in you, and ye need not that any man teach you: but as the same anointing teacheth you of all things, and is truth, and is no lie, and even as it hath taught you, ye shall abide in him.'

The term *anointing* (*chrisma*) is the word from which the title 'Christ' derives. Christ is the anointed One; hence, Christians are also anointed ones. As Christ was anointed with the Spirit, so we, too, have an 'unction from the holy one'. God has not only given us his Word; he has also given us his Spirit. The Spirit comes to indwell every believer.

Jesus describes this Spirit in John 16 as 'the Spirit of truth'. If you are a believer, the Spirit who dwells inside you makes you sensitive to everything that is honouring to Christ and to anything that is dishonouring to Christ. When we hear false teaching, the Spirit provides understanding and illumination, enabling you to discern truth from error.

When John says in verse 27, 'The anointing which ye have received of him abideth in you, and ye need not that any man teach you', he is not telling us that we don't need to be taught the things of God. That would contradict everything else he says in this epistle. Rather, John is saying, 'I am writing about those who are trying to lead you astray, yet you do not need anyone to teach you that because the Holy Spirit has already alerted you to the error of what they are teaching. Heed the Spirit's warning.'

The Holy Spirit alerts us to false teaching that sweeps through the world and changes with the age. Errors come and go. People are enamoured with them until something else comes along. Then the next generation looks back and asks, 'How could you believe such things?' By contrast, the Christian remains anchored in the truth because he has God's Word and his Spirit and they always operate in harmony. The Spirit of God does not contradict the Word of God.

According to John, the ultimate end of the Word and Spirit is not merely that we have right notions, but that we abide in Christ: 'even as it [the anointing Spirit] hath taught you, ye shall abide in him [Christ]' (v. 27). The aim of false teachers is to separate us from Christ, while the purpose of the gospel is to bring us to Christ. The whole point of the Bible is not to correct

our minds and give us right notions about God, as important as
these things are, but to bring us into, and preserve us in, a saving relationship with Christ.

Antichrists abound in our world today. Recently, world leaders met to discuss developing a constitution for a United Europe. When confronted with the question about God's place in
the constitution, a few leaders said that God must have some
place because belief in him is foundational to European culture.
But the majority of leaders said that was uncalled for. One even
said it would be stupid. It now appears certain that there will be
no mention of God in the European constitution.

Did you know that in certain parts of Europe, it is now
against the law to preach Jesus Christ outdoors if only one person objects? Christians have been arrested and thrown in prison
in England because they would not stop preaching.

Matters are not much better in America. Even a God-fearing
president can scarcely dare to make direct references to Jesus
Christ in his speeches. Meantime, pressure is intensifying against
Christians around the globe. International Socialism or Com-
munism is militantly atheistic, and still wars against the Christian
faith in China today. Islam is likewise profoundly antichristian,
and enslaves millions at the present time. In many countries,
Christians whose lives are being threatened by imprisonment
and death are clinging to Christ's promise, 'He that endureth to
the end shall be saved' (Matt. 10:22). The secret of such endur-
ance is to abide in Christ, in the light of his Word and the power
of the Holy Spirit.

# 11

# *Abiding in Christ*

*And now, little children, abide in him; that, when he shall appear, we may have confidence, and not be ashamed before him at his coming. If ye know that he is righteous, ye know that every that doeth righteousness is born of him* (1 John 2:28–29).

Summing up what he has said so far, John exhorts believers to abide in Christ. The word *abide* means to dwell in, to continue, to be faithful, to stand firm. Abiding in Christ means at least five things.

## What Abiding in Christ Means

First, abiding in Christ means receiving Christ by faith and continuing in Christ by faith. But before continuing in Christ, we must first get into Christ. Faith brings us into that saving union with Christ. Some of us need to begin here. We must ask ourselves: Have we truly believed in Christ, embraced him in our hearts, trusted him, received him as God's provision for our sin, and do we now wish to live in constant dependence upon him?

Second, abiding in Christ means continuing in his Word. John has already said that in verse 24: 'Let that therefore abide in you, which ye have heard from the beginning. If that which ye have heard from the beginning shall remain in you, ye also shall continue in the Son, and in the Father.' In other words, you continue in Christ as you hold fast to his truth, his promises, his encouragements, his warnings, and his precepts.

If you are to continue in Christ, so that you will be 'confident and unashamed' (v. 28) when he comes again to this earth, you must sink your life into God's truth and be nourished by it. The Bible is the food that God has given to nourish our souls. It is vital to our spiritual well being and growth. Feed upon God's Word; allow it to teach, train, and guide you. Abide in Christ by abiding in his Word.

Third, abiding in Christ means communing with him through the sacraments he has appointed for our use. God's sacraments complement his Word. They point us away from ourselves to God. Each sign — water, bread, and wine — directs us to Christ as the source for godly living. The sacraments are visible means through which Christ communes with us, and we with him.

Fourth, abiding in Christ means leaning on the work of God's Spirit. In verse 27, John reminds us that God has given us his Holy Spirit. The Spirit protects us from error by illuminating our minds to recognize and understand the truth, and moving our hearts to embrace it and cling to it.

Finally, abiding in Christ means abiding in the fellowship of his church. That involves loving our brothers and sisters in Christ, even to the point of being willing to lay down our lives for them for Christ's sake, as we will see more fully in 1 John 3:14-18.

## Why Abiding in Christ is Important

In verses 28 and 29, John offers us the greatest encouragement to be faithful and true to Jesus Christ. He has been encouraging Christians to persevere in the faith, and here he gives them an important reason why they should do so. He says, 'And now, little children, abide in him; that, when he shall appear, we may have confidence [the word *confidence* here means to be bold, open faced, to speak freely] and not be ashamed before him at his coming.'

Notice that John speaks here of the second coming of Jesus Christ. He is telling Christians that history has an end point and that all of us have an appointment from which not even death can keep us. That end point is the personal, visible, glorious appearing of the Lord Jesus Christ. Life is not an unending series of timeless events, nor an endlessly repeating cycle, nor something that can be snuffed out in some cosmic cataclysm. History has a God-appointed destiny. The Creator who made all things has also decreed the end of all things. That end will come with the appearing of Jesus Christ. And 'When he shall appear [literally, "when he is unveiled and set before us"], we may have confidence, and not be ashamed before him at his coming.'

This truth echoes the teaching of Jesus in the gospels. Prior to being betrayed by Judas, Jesus said, 'And then shall appear the sign of the Son of man in heaven: and then shall all the tribes of the earth mourn, and they shall see the Son of man coming in the clouds of heaven with power and great glory. And he shall send his angels with a great sound of a trumpet, and they shall gather together his elect from the four winds, from one end of heaven to the other' (Matt. 24:30-31). Jesus was looking beyond the cross, the resurrection, and the ascension, to that day when he will return as the Son of God, displayed in all his divine majesty. This is the final act in the drama of redemption, the final event circled on God's calendar. Every day brings us closer to that event that the New Testament mentions 318 times in its 260 chapters.

Because this is where history is heading, we must prepare so that we can meet our Saviour with confidence rather than fear and shame.

Consider a bride preparing for her wedding day. The day for the wedding is circled on the calendar; although it is many months away, she prepares for the event well in advance, so that she can be ready to meet her groom on her wedding day. The last thing a bride wants to do is shrink away from her groom in shame because her gown is soiled or her hair is not combed or her veil is torn. The groom would not be pleased at her lack of preparation. Being unprepared is an indication that true love for the other person is missing, for love stirs the heart to prepare for one's beloved.

Cling to Christ, John says. Adorn your soul with his grace so that you can meet the Bridegroom clothed in beautiful wedding garments of righteousness and holiness, without which no bride shall see the Bridegroom in peace.

Romans 9:33 says, 'Whosoever believeth on him shall not be ashamed.' That means whoever continues to believe in Christ will die in him. Sooner than we think, we will hear the voice of the archangel and the trumpet of God. We will see our Lord coming on the clouds, and we will rise to meet him with joy and gladness. We, who have embraced him as Saviour, are confident that he will accept us because of his own righteousness.

How blessed it will be not to be ashamed when we see Christ! How blessed not to be ashamed of living and dying for him and for the cause of the gospel! How blessed not to be ashamed to embrace him as our Saviour, Lord, Elder Brother, Immanuel! In the day that Jesus returns, we will see how every sorrow, sickness, and trial was designed to bring us to this confident expectation of meeting our God in the clouds.

Spiritually healthy believers long for Christ's Second Coming. John Calvin said, 'If we do not ardently look forward to the second coming of Christ, we have made little progress in the Christian life.' Or as John Cotton put it, 'Do you love and pray for his coming? ... The day of judgement is a day of marriage to the godly, and therefore the spouse longs for it; but to the wicked it is a day of execution, and therefore they tremble at the thought and hearing of it' (*First John*, p.300).

Those who once professed Christianity and have now turned away from Christ and from his bride, the church, and are following false teachers will shrink from Christ in terror when he appears in the clouds. They will be ashamed before him because of their wretched choice to forsake the Fountain of living waters for cisterns that hold no water. Their guilty consciences will make them shrink from his holy presence in guilty silence (Rom. 3:19) and with wailing (Rev. 1:7).

If Christ were to come on the clouds today, would you shrink from him or would you fly to him with confidence? Examine yourself, repent of your backsliding, flee again to Christ, and rest confidently in his precious blood.

## Another Mark of Abiding in Christ

John goes on in verse 29 to explain another way of knowing whether we are abiding in Christ. He says, 'If ye know that he is righteous, ye know that every one that doeth righteousness is born of him.' In other words, since you know that the Christ of whom John has been speaking is the Righteous One — the righteous Lord who loves righteousness — it clearly follows that you who have been born of him and abide in him will also do righteousness. He that 'doeth righteousness' is synonymous of the person who abides in Christ. Righteousness here does not refer to imputed, justifying righteousness but to fruit-bearing, sanctifying righteousness.

Righteousness is the inevitable fruit of abiding in Christ; it is the manifestation of abiding in Christ. Abiding in Christ means pursuing Christ's righteousness and gleaning from it the Spirit-worked power to do what is righteous in God's sight.

The antichrists said that knowledge was the great mark of a Christian. They said they were believers because they knew a lot about God. John says the most important mark of God's people is righteousness, not knowledge — though knowledge of the truth is essential to obedience. Continuing in Christ entails a manner of life that exhibits his righteousness.

John emphasizes the principle of creation that everything brings forth fruit 'after his kind'. The parent is reproduced in the child. Likewise, as Jesus says in John 5:19, the Son of man does what the Father does, out of love. Similarly, in John 15, Jesus says that believers are called to keep the Son's commandments out of love and to be like him, just as the Son keeps his Father's commandments out of love. Since Christ is righteous, those born of him must be righteous. The members of Christ's body must be conformed to him in their conduct; the fruit of being like him becomes evident in their nature and character.

What does it mean to live in righteousness? How do we know what is right? Scripture teaches basically three things about living in righteousness:

1. *It is living rightly toward God.* Living righteously means loving God and obeying his law with all our heart. It is loving, obedient living. Obedience was the great hallmark of Jesus' life. He said, 'I am come not to do my own will, but the will of him that sent me.' Though obedience cost Jesus everything, he lovingly pursued the path that the Father set before him. If it meant the reproach of a godless world, or if it meant dying broken and abandoned on a Roman cross, so be it.

   Too often we forget that living in righteousness begins with obedience. By marginalizing God, we reduce right living to being kind to our neighbour. But the Bible makes plain that we can be kind to our neighbour every day of our life and end up in hell if we have ignored God, the mighty Creator. Our first priority in life must be to lovingly obey God. True righteousness is not righteousness for the sake of reward, but the righteousness of a willing servant.

2. *It is living rightly toward others.* This means treating others as God has treated us — generously and mercifully. God has brought us truth. He has given us his Son. Doing what is right means behaving like a member of God's family. You know how people say of a young man, 'You are just like your father; you look like him, and you talk like him.' When people look at a Christian, they should say, 'You resemble your Father in heaven; you do things the way he does them. You talk the way he does. You behave towards others as the Lord commands you.'

   Tragically, sometimes believers sound more like the world than their heavenly Father. My neighbour mistreated me, so I'll get him back, we say. Or, she was not kind to me, so I'll ignore her the next time I see her. Jesus says God is merciful to the righteous and the unrighteous. Living in righteousness means we treat others as God in Christ has treated us.

3. *It is living rightly toward self.* This involves at least two things. First, it means mortification, or putting off the old man (Eph. 4:24), that is, putting to death the sin that lives in us. As Romans 8:13–14 says, 'For if ye live after the flesh, ye shall die: but if ye through the Spirit do mortify the deeds of the body, ye shall live. For as many as are led by the Spirit of God, they are the sons of God.' Right living means choking sin to death in our lives, thereby showing God how seriously we take the sin that nailed the Son of God to the cross of Calvary. As John Owen put it, 'Be killing sin or sin will be killing you.' Second, it means vivification, or putting 'on the new man, which after God is created in righteousness and true holiness' (Eph. 4:24). Living rightly involves *doing* as well as *not doing.* It embraces the positive fight for righteousness as well as the negative battle against unrighteousness. It entails a daily renewal in the spirit of our mind, a daily disposition that moves us to overcome evil with good (Rom. 12:21).

Dear believer, live in a way that gives evidence of your loyalty to Christ. Make him the grand object of your mind and heart, the centre of your affections. Let him be the One with whom you converse daily in prayer. Follow the example he has left you. Seek your deepest joy in him. Strive to become better established in his doctrine and to grow in his grace and knowledge. Strive to live rightly in every sphere of your life — not to earn salvation but to abide in the One who has saved you.

# 12

## Our Glorious Adoption

*Behold, what manner of love the Father hath bestowed upon us, that we should be called the sons of God: therefore the world knoweth us not, because it knew him not. Beloved, now are we the sons of God, and it doth not yet appear what we shall be: but we know that, when he shall appear, we shall be like him; for we shall see him as he is. And every man that hath this hope in him purifieth himself, even as he is pure* (1 John 3:1–3).

John now turns to the important theme of the fatherhood of God and the sonship of believers. We do not have to read far in the New Testament to realize how this relationship should control a believer's entire outlook on life. The revelation of the fatherhood of God to the believer is one of the greatest benefits of salvation.

### The Wonder of Adoption

John begins chapter 3 with a call for believers to drop everything and consider the great doctrine of adoption. 'Behold!' is John's opening cry; 'Look at this!' The apostle is so overwhelmed with the wonder of God's adoption of believers that he is determined to direct everyone's attention there. He asks us to gaze with him upon this wonder: 'Behold, what manner of love the Father hath bestowed upon us that we should be called the sons of God' (v. 1). It is as if John asks, do you know the wonder of this precious truth? Have you, by faith, comprehended this magnificent doctrine of adoption?

John's sense of astonishment is more evident in the original Greek, which implies, 'Behold, from what country or realm does such love as this come?' Matthew 8:27 uses similar phraseology to describe how astonished the disciples were when Jesus calmed the winds and the sea: 'What manner of man is this (literally, "from what realm does this man come") that even the winds and sea obey him!'

God's adoption of believers is something unparalleled in this world. This fatherly love has come upon us from another realm. The world does not understand such love, for it has never seen anything like it. It is beyond the realm of human experience.

John is astonished because God showed such amazing love even though we were sinners, rebels, and enemies against him and his kingdom. God 'calls' us sons of God; that is, he brings us into his family, giving us the name, the privileges, and all the blessings of his own children. He invites us to know him as Father and to dwell under his protection and care, and to come to him with all our cares and needs. John is overwhelmed at the thought of being a full member of God's family.

Do you stand in awe of this wonderful love of the Father? Holy wonder and amazement is an important part of Christian experience. One of the devil's tactics is to dull our sense of wonder, convincing us that we only feel such wonder in the initial stages of becoming a Christian. It is true that the sinner experiences a special sense of joy and wonder when he first comes to know Christ. We often refer to that time as one's 'first love'.

John is writing here as an elderly man who has been a believer for more than sixty years. Yet his heart is still filled with amazement at being a son of God. He has never gotten over his initial sense of wonder at God's fatherly love. He is still asking the question: 'From what realm does this amazing love come that has broken in upon my soul and made me a child of God?'

We must meditate on Scripture if we would have our hearts burn within us. That is what the pilgrims on the way to Emmaus said to each other after Christ had opened Scripture to them. 'Did not our heart burn within us, while he talked with us by the way, and while he opened to us the scriptures?' (Luke 24:32) they asked in astonishment. Is it any wonder that some believers have lost their sense of wonder and amazement over the gospel when they so seldom study the Bible prayerfully and meditatively?

**The Grace of Adoption**

Believers are not sons of God by nature. We lost the status and privileges of sonship in our tragic fall in Paradise. Adoption is only made possible when God's gracious choice calls us into all the privileges and blessings of being his children. When we are born again, God delivers us from Satan's slavery, and by his astounding grace, transfer us to the Father's sonship. He calls us sons; we are adopted into his family.

Adoption in the time of John usually took place in adolescence or adulthood, not infancy. Under Roman law, adoption was a legal act by which a man chose someone outside of the family to be an heir to his inheritance. Likewise, believers become children of God through the gracious act of God the Father, who chooses them to be his heirs, and joint heirs with Christ.

'Beloved, now are we the sons of God', says John in verse 2. How astonishing that we as God's adopted children share the same privileges that belong to God's only-begotten Son! Have you grasped what Christ prays in John 17: 'The love with which thou hast loved me, thou hast loved them'? This love is the essence of God's fatherhood. It shows us how far God is willing to go to reconcile us to himself.

How great is the love the Father has lavished on us that we should be called children of God — we who deserve his judgement, dethroned him from our lives, spurned his love, and defied his laws. We never deserve God's love, yet he graciously lavishes love upon us in Christ. Here, surely, is the great assurance of the child of God, that God the Father loved him when he was bound for hell. God loved the sinner who had no thought of God in his heart, and God adopted him to be his. Oh, what wonder is the assurance of the Father's words: 'I have loved thee with an everlasting love' (Jer. 31:3).

All the members of the Trinity are involved in our adoption. Adoption is the gracious act of God the Father whereby he chooses us, calls us to himself, and gives us the privileges and blessings of being his children. God the Son earned those blessings for us through his propitiatory death and sacrifice, by which we become children of God (1 John 4:10). And the Holy Spirit changes us from children of wrath, which we are by nature, into children of God by means of regeneration and seals our sonship.

In 1 John 2:29, the apostle explains the relationship between regeneration and adoption. If in adoption we would only receive the privilege and status of being God's children, something would still be missing. The adopted child retains the nature of his natural parents, not the nature of the adoptive parents. God, in his amazing grace, not only gives us the status and privileges of being his children by adoption, but he also gives us the Spirit of sonship, which abides within us by Spirit-worked regeneration. The Holy Spirit implants a new nature within us. As 1 John 3:9 says, 'Whosoever is born of God doth not commit sin [no one born of God goes on committing sin]; for his seed remaineth in him [for a new nature abides in him].'

Are you a child of God? Do you know what it means to have a new nature that cries out for the living God and lives under his fatherly love, fellowship, and protection? Have you been transferred from Satan's slavery to the Father's sonship by God's astounding grace?

## The Blessings of Adoption

Adoption brings blessings into every part of a believer's life. It affects his relationship to God, to the world, to his future, to himself, and to brothers and sisters in God's family. The biblical doctrine of adoption is central to a proper understanding of every major area of the Christian's life.

Christ himself is the best proof of this truth. Jesus' consciousness of his unique sonship with the Father controlled all of Christ's living and thinking. As Jesus says in John 5:30, 'I seek not mine own will, but the will of my Father which hath sent me', and in John 10:30, 'I and my Father are one.' 'If I do not the works of my Father, believe me not', Jesus says in John 10:37, and 'As my Father hath sent me, even so send I you' (John 20:21). More than thirty times in the gospel of John Jesus speaks of 'my Father'.

Jesus likewise urges his disciples to let their thoughts and lives be controlled by the conviction that God is now their Father and they are his children. He tells his disciples that they are to be examples of trusting their Father, asking them, 'Why are you anxious about what you should eat or drink or about your future — your Father knows that you have need of all these things.' Because their whole lives must be directed to do their Father's glory and obey his will, Jesus teaches his disciples to pray: 'Our Father which art in heaven, hallowed by thy name, thy kingdom come, thy will be done, on earth as it is in heaven.' The child of God is to live his whole life in relation to his Father, remembering that the Father has promised each child his kingdom.

Practically speaking, the significance of adoption has great implications. It affects the following:

1. *Our relationship to God.* People are hungry for security today. They look for it in the wrong places, and often go about it the wrong way. The only place in the universe where true security can to be found is in the household of the heavenly Father, who is the God and Father of our Lord Jesus Christ. There is no way to that security outside of believing on the Father and the Son.

    Many people are discovering that the things that once gave them security are now falling apart. They are facing failure in business, jobs, or relationships with family members and friends. They are beset with financial insolvency, terrorism, and war. So much in life is uncertain; so much is crumbling away. The most powerful company on earth may fold in the next recession. We learn that nothing in life is secure except God. He alone does not change (Mal. 3:6).

Are you looking for security in the fatherhood of God? Are you daily being led deeper into his faithfulness as your Father? Jesus taught his disciples this truth in many ways. For example, he urged them to think about God's fatherly love by comparing it to the love of a human father: 'If ye then, being evil, know how to give good gifts to your children, how much more shall your Father which is in heaven give good things to them that ask him?' (Matt. 7:11).

The comparison is between the fatherhood of earthly fathers, who are evil (i.e., they have fallen natures and show flaws and failures and sins) and the fatherhood of God, who is steadfast in love that never falters or changes, even when we sin. God's fatherhood is flawless. I will show you a love, says Jesus, which is expansive and glorious beyond imagination. It is the love of your Father in heaven.

I don't know what your experience of human fatherhood has been. Some of us have had little relationship with our earthly fathers; some have had good experiences, and others have had disappointing, even bitter, experiences. Everything that fails in human fatherhood is corrected in God's fatherhood. Everything good we experience in human fatherhood is a mere shadow of the full and perfect fatherhood of God.

To increase his people's appreciation for God's fatherhood, Jesus urges his people to think of his own relationship to God the Father. We need to ponder the wonder of this especially in the context of daily afflictions, remembering that Jesus felt his Father's love in the afflictions he underwent. When you are under God's discipline and he is permitting trials to fall upon you, remember that even these difficulties are evidence of your Father's love (Heb. 12:5–11). God has a plan, a purpose, a vision for his people as a loving Father that embraces every affliction and heartache.

God knows how he will mould and train them according to his plan, and inevitably, that involves discipline because God will not permit his people to be less than what he intends them to be. He uses his fatherly discipline for their welfare (Lam.3:31–33; Heb. 12:5-14).

2.  *Our relationship to the world.* The believer's adoption by God the Father also affects his relationship to the world. First John 3:1b tells us that this relationship is a troubled one: 'therefore the world knoweth us not, because it knew him not'. On the one hand, the believer shares with Jesus the unspeakable love of the Father, but on the other hand, he shares with Jesus the hostility, estrangement, and even hatred of the world. The reason the world does not know the children of God is because it does not know Jesus. This reaction of the world is evidence of the believer's adoption into God's family, for the world did not know Jesus either; he came unto his own and his own received him not. He was in the world, which was created by him, but the world knew him not. The world did not recognize him as the Son of God; ultimately, it crucified him.

    When a sinner is born again and brought into God's family, he comes to know the great blessings of deliverance in Christ. But the believer also discovers that worldly people no longer understand him. For example, when God converted me at age fourteen, I had to break some of my closest friendships to remain faithful to God. One friend was puzzled. 'I thought I knew you, but I do not know what has happened to you', he said. 'I cannot understand you. Suddenly we are living in two different worlds.'

Believers and unbelievers live in different worlds, in different kingdoms, in different families. That cannot help but bring consequences. But adoption into God's family means that we must be willing for Christ's sake to walk in the world even if we are misunderstood, unwanted, despised, even hated, all the while giving no unnecessary offence to the world.

3.  *Our relationship to the future.* We cherish a great hope. John goes on to say, 'Beloved, now are we the sons of God, and it doth not yet appear what we shall be: but we know that, when he shall appear, we shall be like him; for we shall see him as he is' (1 John 3:2). The prospects for God's adopted family are great, for his children will receive a glorious inheritance. They cannot even imagine the extent of that inheritance.

God's child is like a poor peasant who has been taken out of the mire and raised to the position of prince of the realm. The adopted prince lives in the palace, has free access to the king, and enjoys the king's favour, love, and protection. The prince tells the king he cannot comprehend the greatness of the king's love. It is unspeakably great to him. The king responds: 'You have not begun to see the extent of it. Your inheritance is still coming to you.'

If our present privileges as God's adopted children are so great that the world cannot grasp them, our future prospects are so glorious that even we cannot fully grasp them. As 1 Corinthians 2:9 says, 'Eye hath not seen, nor ear heard, neither have entered into the heart of man, the things which God hath prepared for them that love him.' Because God is our Father and we are his adopted children, we have a full inheritance awaiting us. The best is yet to be. Today we experience great blessings, despite our infirmities and sins, but one day we shall be in glory, free from sin and living in perfect communion with God. Our heavenly Father keeps the best surprises for his children until the end, when he shall turn all their sorrow into joy.

Likewise, today we look at Christ by faith. Though what we see is shadowy and dim, we are being changed from glory to glory by the Spirit of the Lord (2 Cor. 3:18). One day all shadows will be removed. We will see Christ as he is, in all his glory. Moreover, God is shaping us to share in the glories of our Lord Jesus Christ. As 1 John 3:2 says, 'When he shall appear, we shall be like him; for we shall see him as he is.' God is changing us now, but then we shall be so changed that we will fully bear his image without spot or wrinkle. Paul tells us in Romans 8 that the whole creation waits for the day when the inheritance of the children of God will be given to them. What a future!

4. *Our relationship to ourselves.* The children of the heavenly Father embrace his will and purpose for them. Every adopted child of God also knows that holiness is an important part of God's purpose for his happiness in God's family. As 1 John 3:3 says, 'And every man that hath this hope in him purifieth himself, even as he is pure.'

So we are to purify ourselves daily. As Colossians 3 tells us, holiness means putting off everything that is dishonouring to our Father, who has loved us, and the Saviour, who has died to save us. It means putting on 'mercies, kindness, humbleness of mind, meekness, and longsuffering' (3:12). Purifying ourselves involves what we do with our minds, thoughts, tongue, eyes, hands, disappointments, injuries, and enemies. Purifying ourselves involves loving all that the Father loves and hating all that the Father hates. From the moment of conversion to the time we take our final breath, we have one pursuit: to purify ourselves before our Father in order to be more like Christ.

The Greek word for *purify* refers to undivided allegiance, or having one's eyes on one thing. It implies wholeness and singleness of purpose. It means having undivided motives in our living and our service, being wholly dedicated to living to glorify Jesus Christ. The way that Christians become known as sons of God is that they have a new goal for themselves, a new relationship toward themselves. By God's grace, they purify themselves even as Christ is pure.

5.  *Our relationship to the church family of God.* As God's adopted sons and daughters, we have been placed in a great family. If we rightly understand this, our attitude toward our brothers and sisters in the family of God will be profoundly affected (3:14–18). We have not been adopted to live apart from that family but to live within it as a network of relationships. God's purpose in adopting children is to create a family, in which Christ will be glorified as the firstborn among many brethren. He wants the love that exists between the Father and the Son and the Holy Spirit to be extended through the love between brothers and sisters in Christ.

    The communion of saints is essential to the proclamation and vindication of the gospel. That is why it is so grievous when people in the church do not show love to one another. If we profess a Saviour that laid down his life for us and we are part of his family, we ought to be willing to lay down our lives for other members of the family. We should uphold them, serve them, and sacrifice for them. We should not grieve each other, wound each other, or gossip about each other. The way we behave toward other Christians proves whether or not we are adopted children of God (3:14–15).

    If we show little love to other children of God, we prove that we have tasted little of God's love in our life, for those who have experienced much love from him cannot help but love others. Those who have not known the love of God will not love the brethren.

# 13

# The Contrast Between
# Righteousness and Sin

*Whosoever committeth sin transgresseth also the law:
for sin is the transgression of the law. And ye know that
he was manifested to take away our sins; and in him
is no sin. Whosoever abideth in him sinneth not: whosoever sinneth hath not seen him, neither known him.
Little children, let no man deceive you: he that doeth
righteousness is righteous, even as he is righteous. He
that committeth sin is of the devil; for the devil sinneth
from the beginning. For this purpose the Son of God
was manifested, that he might destroy the works of the
devil. Whosoever is born of God doth not commit sin;
for his seed remaineth in him: and he cannot sin, because he is born of God. In this the children of God
are manifest, and the children of the devil: whosoever
doeth not righteousness is not of God, neither he that
loveth not his brother* (1 John 3:4–10).

First John 3:4 through 4:6 addresses the themes of righteousness,
love, faith, and truth again, but this time sets them before us
in terms of contrasts: righteousness and sin (3:4–10), love
and hate (3:11–18), faith and doubt (3:19–24), and truth and
error (4:1–6). John's goal throughout this section is to sharpen

the distinction between true and false believers by showing
how their lives differ. The false teachers or Gnostics who had
infiltrated the early Christian church spoke with eloquence and
passion, but their lives failed to show the true marks of grace:
righteousness, love, faith, and truth.

This theme was introduced in 1 John 1:6, 'If we say that
we have fellowship with God and Christ, and walk in darkness,
we lie, and do not the truth.' In other words, if we say that we
are Christian people but do not live by the standards of God's
Word, then our lives betray us. We lie, and the truth is not in
us.

## The Seriousness of Sin

John reminds us, first, of the seriousness of sin. He highlights
two things. First, he addresses the nature of sin: 'Whosoever
committeth sin transgresseth also the law, for sin is the transgression of the law' (v. 4). Some people define sin as something
that spoils our lives. That is true; when we step outside of God's
ways, we should not be surprised if sin spoils things. But the
Bible teaches us that sin is much deeper than that. The New
Testament uses at least four words to describe sin:

1. *Hamartia.* This word means missing the mark, or falling
   short of the target. An archer takes a bow and arrow
   and aims at a target, but somehow the arrows keep going awry and he misses his mark. Likewise, we fall short
   of that mark which is the goal of God's chief end for
   man, namely, to glorify God. By nature, every one of us
   misses the target, as Paul stresses in Romans (3:9; 5:12,
   20).

2. *Adikia* is usually translated unrighteousness, or sometimes iniquity (Luke 16:8; Rom. 1:18, 29; 2:8). The
   word brings up the image of a straight or level edge. A
   bricklayer sets up bricks in a row, occasionally placing
   a level on the bricks to make sure they are straight. In a

similar way, God's perfect righteousness offers a straight edge to man for how he should live. When our lives are measured against God's straight edge, they do not square up. They are not on the level.

3. *Paraptomah* means an offense or fault, or something done outside the bounds God has set for our conduct. God has a road for man to travel. Travel regulations include white lines, double yellow lines, and various road signs. We keep violating those road signs. We regard God's road as too narrow or too restrictive so we try other, broader roads, which lie alongside God's road.

    Jesus describes the way we should travel in Matthew 7. 'Strait is the gate, and narrow is the way' God has for us. His road leads to life, even though 'few there be that find it' (v. 14). Jesus warns us about forsaking the right way, saying, 'Enter ye in at the strait gate: for wide is the gate, and broad is the way, that leadeth to destruction, and many there be which go in thereat' (v. 13). Worldly people prefer the broad road rather than the narrow one.

4. *Anomia* means transgression of law, lawlessness, or literally, having 'no law'. John uses this word in 1 John 3:4. As King and Ruler of creation, God has given us laws to live by, which are summarized in the Ten Commandments. We have rebelled against those laws, but not merely by going astray. Sin is more than being a prodigal who has wandered from his father's house. We deliberately rebel, not only against divine laws, but against the divine Lawgiver. Instead of submitting to God's rule and authority, we want to be a law unto ourselves. Sin is man's refusal to submit his mind, heart, and will to the authority of God. He does not want anyone other than himself to be lord of his life.

    Sin is anti-God; it is treason against the Most High. It strikes out against God's holiness and glory; in fact, it

flies in the face of every attribute of God. As John Bunyan said, 'Sin is the daring of God's justice, the jeering
of his patience, the slighting of his power, the contempt
of his love.'

Second, John addresses the origin of sin. 'He that committeth sin is of the devil; for the devil sinneth from the beginning'
(v. 8). What a radical statement that is. Though we might wonder if the apostle is being extreme, we must realize this is not just
John's perspective; it is God's perspective on sin.

Jesus once said to certain religious leaders of his day, 'Ye
are of your father, the devil, and the lusts of your father ye will
do' (John 8:44a). The leaders recoiled from the accusation as
darkness recoils from the burning light of the sun. Sin originates
in hell. Its intent is to blind people to the God who made them
and to the Saviour who came to redeem them. Every time we
numb ourselves to sin or are tempted to trivialize and excuse it,
we must remember, 'Sin is of the devil.'

If you are a Christian, one of the evidences of your Christian
faith is your attitude to sin. Sins that you once considered triv-
ial now plunge like arrows into your heart. Language that you
once used freely now makes you think, 'That language ill befits
someone who claims to be a child of the holy God of heaven!'
John reminds us of these things because we will never seek a
remedy until we are persuaded in our minds and hearts how
seriously ill we are. God's concern is not simply to make us feel
bad and guilty about ourselves. He wants to bring us to the end
of ourselves so that we cry out, 'What must I do to be saved?'

Do you notice that righteousness and sin are opposites?
John makes that plain in verses 6 and 7: 'Whosoever abideth in
him sinneth not: whosoever sinneth hath not seen him, neither
known him. Little children, let no man deceive you: he that
doeth righteousness is righteous, even as he is righteous.'

## The Twofold Purpose of Christ's Incarnation

John explains the purpose of Christ's incarnation in terms of
two contrasts. First, Christ came into the world *to take away our*

*sins.* So John says of believers in verse 5, 'Ye know that he was manifested [i.e., he came, or he appeared] to take away our sins.' That confirms the angel's message to Joseph, 'Thou shalt call his name JESUS; for he shall save his people from their sins' (Matt. 1:21).

God sent his sinless Son to earth to satisfy divine justice through Christ's obedience — his active obedience in fulfilling the law and his passive obedience in paying the price of sin submissively. He did so to satisfy the claims of divine justice against believers and so that believers can be separated from the sin that has become such a major part of us. Christ takes that sin away. Psalm 103:12 says, 'As far as the east is from the west, so far hath he removed our transgressions from us.'

Because of the spotless Lamb of God, who paid for our sins in his own body on the accursed tree at Golgotha, God delights to cast our sins behind him into the sea of eternal forgetfulness. Because Christ died in our place, our sin will never be remembered against us or visited upon us. What wonderful salvation! What magnificent blessing!

Consider the lengths to which God is willing to go to deal with sin — the very thing that would keep you from communion with God and from heaven (Isa. 59:2; Rev. 21:8). Jesus is God's remedy for sin — could anything be more important than that? Is not this the good news that each of us yearns to know? However much we evade the issue, there are times when human frailty presses upon us, and we know that the one thing that really matters is that when we leave this life, we leave it as forgiven, reconciled, heaven-bound sinners. All that matters then, is how God views us, not how the world views us.

Second, Jesus came *to destroy the devil's work*. John says in verse 8, 'For this purpose the Son of God was manifested, that he might destroy the works of the devil.' Jesus came not only to take away our sins but also to destroy the lord of sin and the kingdom of evil he has laboured to build.

The devil is no fantasy. He is real. On the cross Christ invaded the territory of darkness to destroy its power. Of course, the devil is still present, and he still roars loudly, but he is a broken, defeated power. His doom is sealed.

On the cross Christ crushed the head and broke the back of Satan. That is why 1 John 4:4 says, 'Ye are of God, little children, and have overcome them: because greater is he that is in you, than he that is in the world.' Through salvation we are taken out of the dominion of Satan into the kingdom of the Son of God.

Christ came to this world to destroy sin and establish righteousness; he himself is the contrast between righteousness and sin. John says at the end of verse 5: 'in him is no sin'. Christ is pure righteousness. He will bring that contrast into believers' lives also, though imperfectly now, perfectly hereafter. Christ's victory over Satan bears astonishing fruits in the lives of those who are born again as his righteousness gains the victory over sinful depravity.

## The Fruit of the New Birth

John goes on to say in verse 9, 'Whosoever is born of God doth not commit sin; for his seed remaineth in him: and he cannot sin, because he is born of God.' John is not saying that Christians never sin. That would contradict 1 John 1:8: 'If we say that we have no sin, we deceive ourselves, and the truth is not in us.' What John is saying is that if God has broken into your life and you now live in Christ by faith, you will not go on living as you once lived. God's 'seed of regeneration' remains in you so you cannot go on sinning. John uses the image of a seed to show that what God plants in the human heart will surely produce a new life, a new disposition, and a new will. You may still sin, but sin will be contrary to the bent of your new life. You will not be content to continue in sin.

This interpretation of verse 9 makes sense, first, because of John's use of the present progressive tense. He literally says: 'No one who *continues to* live in sin has seen or known God; no one who is born of God will go on living in sin because God's seed — the seed of the new birth, a seed that is perfect — remains in him.'

Second, John is writing against the Gnostics who claimed great spiritual insights while living immorally. Though these false teachers made great claims, their lives betrayed them. They reasoned that a person could *be* righteous without having to *practise* righteousness, so John emphasizes that anyone who has been born of God will not be content to go on living in sin. 'If any man be in Christ, he is a new creature: old things are passed away; behold, all things are become new' (2 Cor. 5:17).

Christians still sin, sometimes grievously, but when they sin, it brings sorrow beyond words to their heart. It cuts them to the quick. It brings them to their knees. They say, 'How could I — so loved and forgiven, so precious to God who gave his Son for me — have said that sinful word, or done that sinful act, or indulged that sinful thought?'

Since there is a whole new direction to the lives of those who are born again, the question becomes: How can I now live to please him who gave his Son for my sin? Those who are born again want their new lives to be a seamless tapestry of obedience out of gratitude for what God has done for them in Christ Jesus.

Third, consider how John uses contrasts to make a point. He sets truths forth in a combination of thesis and antithesis. Unlike Paul, who presents the thesis and the antithesis, then works out the synthesis of the two (see Romans 6 and 7), John lets the reader work out the synthesis. For example, in John 1:11, John says, 'He came unto his own, and his own received him not.' Then, in verse 12, he says, 'But as many as received him, to them gave he power to become the sons of God, even to them that believe on his name.' Is John contradicting himself? No, he is setting up a contrast. He does not mean to say in verse 11 that *every* single Jew rejected Jesus. Obviously that is not true, or Jesus would not have had Jewish disciples and apostles. But in general the Jews rejected Jesus. In verse 12, John goes on to speak about those who did receive Jesus.

Here is how John wants us to work out the synthesis in 1 John 3:9. John is not saying that believers have no sin. Rather, he is saying that sin no longer is the bent of their life. Moreover, the new seed within believers cannot sin. Consequently, even though believers still sin due to the remnants of their old nature, they do not live under the dominion of sin. Sin is no longer satisfying to them. Sin has lost its lustre. They no longer want to live in it.

Yet, as Luther said, 'They are righteous, yet sinners.' The power of remaining or indwelling sin brings believers into holy warfare, as Paul so poignantly describes in Romans 7. They must never excuse that pollution. They do not trivialize sin, like the world does; they cannot live untroubled by it. They know that continuing in sin would oppose the whole purpose of Christ's coming to take away sin. To continue in sin is to fight on the wrong side of the cosmic battle against sin.

What is the bent of your life? Do you go on committing sin in comfort and ease? Or do you yearn toward righteousness in Christ? Do you wish with all your heart that all sin was dead in you? Here is the ultimate test that John offers: Do we find our life in Christ's righteousness, and out of his righteousness do righteousness, or do we find our life in sin, and out of the devil's and our own unrighteousness continue committing sin? Are we refusing to surrender our entire lives — including our thought lives — to God?

John says in verse 10, 'In this the children of God are manifest, and the children of the devil: whosoever doeth not righteousness is not of God, neither he that loveth not his brother.' There are two kinds of people in the world, John says: the children of God and the children of the devil. Both are known by how they live. You know who the children of God are because they do what is right. Their lives show they love Christ and obey God. They are increasingly becoming like Christ. Through Christ's righteousness, believers become righteous and obedient from within, then bring forth fruits of righteousness in thoughts, words, and actions.

People serve only two kinds of rulers, divine or diabolical. The world sees all kinds of perspectives in between, but only God's perspective is significant, for the perspectives of the world will fade into oblivion. The only opinion that will stand to the end is that of the eternal, uncreated Triune God. In other words, one of the sins in which the Christian must not go on living is the sin of hatred — hating God by despising his laws, or hating his brethren by withholding from them his compassion.

Ask yourself: Am I convicted of the heinous nature of all sin, including my own? Have I learned to rest by faith in Christ's righteousness, which opposes sin? Am I persuaded of the incompatibility of continuing in sin while living as a Christian?

# 14

## Loving One Another

*For this is the message that ye heard from the beginning,*
*that we should love one another. Not as Cain, who was*
*of that wicked one, and slew his brother. And wherefore*
*slew he him? Because his own works were evil, and*
*his brother's righteous. Marvel not, my brethren, if the*
*world hate you. We know that we have passed from*
*death unto life, because we love the brethren. He that*
*loveth not his brother abideth in death. Whosoever ha-*
*teth his brother is a murderer: and ye know that no mur-*
*derer hath eternal life abiding in him. Hereby perceive*
*we the love of God, because he laid down his life for*
*us: and we ought to lay down our lives for the brethren.*
*But whoso hath this world's good, and seeth his brother*
*have need, and shutteth up his bowels of compassion*
*from him, how dwelleth the love of God in him? My*
*little children, let us not love in word, neither in tongue;*
*but in deed and truth* (1 John 3:11–18).

The meaning of love has been seriously diluted eroded today.
Practically everyone claims to love God. Everyone who claims
to be Christian also claims to love God and his neighbor. But
true love is much deeper than emotion, sentimentality, infatu-
ation, or a carnal love that indulges the flesh. John tells us in
1 John 3:11–18 what true love is and how it differs from hate,

showing us the origin, nature, and practical consequences of both.

## Commanded to Love

In explaining the meaning of love, John says the commandment to love is hardly news to his listeners. You have had the message of the 'royal law' (James 2:8) from the beginning, he says. In 1 John 2:7, we examined how John reminded believers that they had 'heard from the beginning' the old commandment which had now taken on new meaning. The same thing applies here. John is referring to the words of Jesus, 'A new commandment I give unto you, That ye love one another; as I have loved you, that ye also love one another. By this shall all men know that ye are my disciples, if ye have love one to another' (John 13:34–35).

It is striking that Jesus commands us to love, since most people do not think of love as a response to a command. We think about love being an instinctive or emotional response or an inclination, but Jesus elevates love by linking it with the command to love God and one's neighbour. Love is not an option for a Christian; love is not to be held hostage by our changing emotions. Love is an attitude that we cultivate and a pattern of behaviour that we embrace.

Jesus and the New Testament writers presented love as an essential mark of a saving relationship with God. Love gave strength and credibility to the New Testament witness. When the disciples went into the world, speaking of Christ and living for him, people looked at them and said, 'Behold how they love one another!' That kind of love the world could not ignore; it gave weight to their words. Tertullian, the early church father, said that love made Christianity triumph over persecution in the ancient world. Love is still one of the church's most powerful evangelistic weapons today.

Even so, John presents loving one another as the evidence of true faith in Christ, not as an argument for it. Jesus and other apostles, such as James, Peter, and Paul, handle it the same way. When Jesus and the apostles explained how Christians should behave in the world, they did not begin with arguments. Of course, they did teach us how to live. Scripture is filled with counsel and direction on Christian living, ethics, and morality. But that is not where the apostles began.

John follows the typical apostolic approach. He does not first come with a command, saying, 'You have to be good children; you must love one another and live in harmony with one another. If you fail to do that, you will not be effective.' Rather, John, Jesus, and the apostles handled the command to love in the context of describing believers who already love one another because they are Christians. We must be believers first, then live out that belief in an ever increasing measure of love, they say.

## Love and Hate Contrasted

John goes on to illustrate how to love by contrasting love and hate in verses 12-15. In that framework, he tells us four things: (1) what a Christian is not and (2) what a Christian is; (3) what a Christian does and (4) what a Christian does not do.

1. *What a Christian is not.* John says in verses 12 and 13: 'Not as Cain, who was of that wicked one, and slew his brother. And wherefore slew he him? Because his own works were evil, and his brother's righteous. Marvel not, my brethren, if the world hate you.' John is saying that if a Christian is no longer a man of this world, he will not act like Cain, who personified this world and hated his brother Abel. Cain is the exemplar of the non-believer, for he was of the wicked one, his works were evil, he abode in death, and he hated his brother. John is drawing a parallel between Cain and the world, and Abel and the Christian.

   You remember the story (Gen. 4:1-8). Abel came to God with his offering. He brought a lamb to God, and God was pleased with the sacrifice. Cain brought the fruit of the field to God as an offering. God was not pleased with that offering. When Cain found that

Abel's offering was accepted, his hatred and resentment so increased against his brother that he murdered him. That has been the relationship of the world to the living church ever since. As Jesus said, 'Do not marvel if the world hates you; it has hated me before it hated you. That is the reason why it hates you.' Cain hated Abel because he hated the light that shone through Abel's life. Likewise, the world hates Christians because it hates the light and the deeds of light.

2.  *What a Christian is.* John tells us in verse 14 what a true Christian is: 'We know that we have passed from death unto life, because we love the brethren.' A true Christian has passed from death unto life. The chief characteristic of this world is that it rests in the lap of the wicked one. It is under the dominion of Satan as the god of this world. As a result of sin, this world in which we are born and live is a realm of spiritual darkness and death. We have been shaped in iniquity and born in sin. Because of that we are part of the realm of death.

    Adam and Eve were given a clear alternative in the Garden of Eden. God commanded them not to eat the fruit of the tree of the knowledge of good and evil. He warned them: 'In the day that thou eatest thereof thou shalt surely die' (Gen. 2:17). Adam and Eve chose to disobey God and took fruit from the tree. As a consequence, sin entered into the world, and death by sin. So, as Paul says, death is cast upon all men for 'all have sinned, and come short of the glory of God' (Rom. 3:22).

    In Ephesians 2:1 Paul said, 'And you hath he quickened, who were dead in trespasses and sins.' To be dead in sin means to be dead to God's realm. It means to be dead to the true knowledge of God, dead to living fellowship with God. A Christian is someone who has come to realize the true nature of sin. He recognizes that he is caught up in the midst of a spiritual conflict and that by nature he is under the dominion of sin and Satan. He recognizes the desperate plight of his position. Furthermore, he sees that only God in Christ can deliver him from that plight. He sees the truth of the gospel in Jesus Christ and comes to a personal knowledge of God.

A Christian is born again. He has become alive to God in Christ. He is a child of God and is in living fellowship with God, having become part of the family of God. He has been translated out of this worldly kingdom of death and brought into the family of God's Son. He once lived in darkness and death, but now he lives in light and life eternal. He has eternal life abiding in him.

3.   *What a Christian does.* John focuses here on the critical issue of Christians loving one another. 'We love the brethren', he says (v. 14b). If a Christian has been made a partaker of the life of God and has been brought into the family of God, then he should have an intimate, loving relationship with every other member of that family. Every other believer has become his brother or sister in Christ. If a person has become a new creation in Christ, if the love of God dwells in his heart by the Spirit, and if he has come to love God as his Father through the Father's own love, then he will love his brothers and sisters in Christ with the love that the Holy Spirit has given to him.

Notice that John is not saying, 'If you want to be good Christians you better start loving one another. You must try harder and put more effort into loving one another.' Rather, he says that love for one another is the inevitable outcome of having passed from death unto life and of having God's eternal life within us. The mindset of all true Christians is to love God and their brothers and sisters in the family of God.

4.  *What a Christian does not do.* Notice how the negative
    aspect of the former teaching reinforces what John has
    just said. A Christian does not hate his brother. Hat-
    ing someone, according to the New Testament, is the
    impulse of murder — the wish or desire to destroy, to
    wound, to hurt. Furthermore, the person who fails to
    love his brother is still in the realm of death (v. 14c). As
    John says, 'Whosoever hateth his brother is a murderer;
    and ye know that no murderer hath eternal life abiding
    in him' (v. 15). The man who does not love his brother
    and sister in Christ still lives and moves in the realm of
    death; his failure to love shows that the life of God does
    not abide in his soul.

    Do we love our brothers and sisters in Christ? Or
    do we harbour resentment, bitterness, envy, and jeal-
    ousy against someone who professes to be a Christian?
    We need to face that kind of question now, before it
    is asked of us on Judgement Day, for love will be the
    standard which judges us on that final day. Many peo-
    ple will come to Christ on Judgement Day, professing
    to have served him. 'Lord, have we not done won-
    derful things in thy name?' they will say. Christ will
    respond, 'I never knew you. You were baptized, you
    participated in the Lord's Supper, and you did many
    things for the church, but you never knew what it meant
    to be born again and to partake of this new nature
    which compelled you to love God and one another.'

**Practising Love**

If you ask people what it means to love, you will get many answers. Most explanations will be shallow because relationships
in our world have become shallow. John tells us what it means
to practise love in verses 16–18: 'Hereby perceive we the love
of God, because he laid down his life for us: and we ought to
lay down our lives for the brethren. But whoso hath this world's
good, and seeth his brother have need, and shutteth up his
bowels of compassion from him, how dwelleth the love of God

in him? My little children, let us not love in word, neither in tongue; but in deed and truth.'

John says two things here. First, he says that *love is self-less, self-sacrificial, and enduring.* We know what true love is because Jesus displayed it in laying down his life for us. Jesus is the great example of what it means to love one another before God. He laid aside his comforts, turned his back on his privileges, endured the cross, and bore the judgement of a holy God for the sins of a lost and guilty people. Even as nails were driven into his body, Jesus refused to stop loving those who were torturing him. He appealed to God, saying, 'Father, forgive them; for they know not what they do' (Luke 23:34). If you want to know what love is, says John, let me take you to the cross; there you will see love in all its brilliance and glory. 'Herein is love, not that we loved God, but that he loved us, and sent his Son to be the propitiation for our sins' (1 John 4:10).

No one anywhere has ever loved the way God did at the cross. No one can stop the outpouring of God's love.

True love seeks what is best for the other person, which is, ultimately, eternal life. The Lord Jesus forfeited his own life so that unlovable sinners could have eternal life. He deliberately chose to love them. He wanted the best for those who were obnoxious to him.

In Christ, God loved his people with abounding love. He loved lavishly, giving them everything he had. When God gave his only Son, his bosom Friend from all eternity, he gave the best that he had for the worst he could find — depraved sinners who were his enemies by nature. In loving the unlovable, God subjected his Son to the worst imaginable sufferings. God held nothing in reserve, for he spared not his own Son.

True love is God's love modelled in Christ. God is the ultimate source of all love. To love truly is to love as God loves. Jesus said, 'Love one another as I have loved you.'

What does such love mean in our relationship with others? John says true love means that we are willing to lay down our lives for our brothers and sisters in Christ, just as Christ laid down his life for us. As Paul says, 'Husbands, love your wives, even as Christ also loved the church, and gave himself for it'

(Eph. 5:25). Jesus Christ and his sacrificial love is the model for family love and for love in a Christian congregation. Selfless, sacrificial service for the good of others is to be the defining feature and the model for all of our relationships.

That kind of love is so important because the devil is unceasing in his attempts to kill love in our lives. Usually he does it slowly. We are hurt by someone in the church, and we begin withdrawing from them. Over a period of time, we gather resentments to justify our isolation. We erect barricades around ourselves to keep others out. We become insensitive to other people and their needs.

If love is dying in your heart, go to the cross of Jesus Christ. Pray that drops of his love would rain upon your heart. Only at the cross will we experience the love that God longs to see in the lives of his people. At Calvary, we see sinless love personified in God's Servant laying down his life to bring the blessings of God to the people of God.

Christian love does not wait for others to do something for us and to us, but reaches out to others in need. Christian love offers its all for the good of those we love. For example, a Christian husband, by the grace of God, will say to his wife, 'I would cross oceans to give you what is best for you; I would lay down my life for your good.' Children learn something of the love of God from Scripture, but they also must see it modelled in their parents' lives. If we are not showing the love of God in our homes, we are telling our children every time the Word of God is preached, 'Do not believe it.'

Second, John teaches us that Christian love is evident in *caring for one another*: 'But whoso hath this world's good, and seeth his brother have need, and shutteth up his bowels of compassion from him, how dwelleth the love of God in him? My little children, let us not love in word, neither in tongue; but in deed and in truth' (vv. 17-18). True love is not what the false teachers do, John says. They speak eloquent words but fail to care for others by sharing resources with them. If you have material possessions and fail to have pity on your brother who is in need, how can the love of God be in you? Pity means doing more than saying, 'I will pray for you.' 'Faith without works is dead' (James 2:26). Showing pity to the needy means sharing our money, our goods, our precious time, our friendship, and ourselves with that person in need.

There is a remarkable description in Matthew 9 of a time when our Saviour was in need. Jesus has been off on an intensive evangelistic tour. He had been walking for days over the hot Judean countryside. He was weary and in need of a break. While resting with his disciples, a great crowd appeared out of nowhere. Jesus' disciples wanted to shoo the people away, but Matthew says Jesus looked at the needy people and was 'moved with compassion on them, as sheep having no shepherd'. He put aside his own weariness and ministered to the people in their need.

When we are in church and are receiving a blessing, it is easy to tell ourselves that we love everyone. It is far more difficult to put that love into practice, especially when it means making personal sacrifices for other believers. We must remember what John says: 'My little children, let us not love in word, neither in tongue; but in deed and in truth' (1 John 3:18). That is the evidence that the love of God is in us.

Love within the family of God must be rekindled. To find our way back to such love, we must go back to where love was gloriously displayed in all its magnificence. We must go back to the cross, where the Prince of glory died. There our cold hearts will be humbled and our hardened hearts ploughed up. There love will once more be revived within us. We will only love one another when we realize how greatly we have been loved. That is why John says, 'Beloved, if God so loved us, we ought also to love one another' (1 John 4:11).

We love one another because God is love. If we claim to be part of His family, then something of that likeness will be manifested in our lives. The practical implications of such sacrificial love include the following:

- *Belief without a loving heart is the faith of devils.* James 2:19 tells us, 'If thou believest that there is one God; thou doest well: the devils also believe, and tremble.' Simply believing in God is not enough. The devils believe in God, too, but they lack a loving heart. Let us not think that because our doctrine is right, we are genuine Christians. We can have right doctrine and wrong hearts. In such a case, even our 'orthodoxy' is spurious. John is clear: whoever does not love does not know God, because God is love.

- *We love God because he first loved us.* God does not ask us to manufacture love; rather, he tells us that we will only love as we should when we know how we have been loved from all eternity by a triune God. When the wonder of the love that gave up heaven's glory for rebellious, hell-deserving sinners breaks into your heart and mind, then true love for God and his people will grow in you. Ultimately, the cross is the answer to everything. When we come back to the cross of Christ, we realize how much God has loved us. We find love at the cross which we then extend to others.

## 15

# *How Christians Should Respond to Doubt*

*And hereby we know that we are of the truth, and shall assure our hearts before him. For if our heart condemn us, God is greater than our heart, and knoweth all things. Beloved, if our heart condemn us not, then have we confidence toward God. And whatsoever we ask, we receive of him, because we keep his commandments, and do those things that are pleasing in his sight. And this is his commandment, that we should believe on the name of his Son Jesus Christ, and love one another, as he gave us commandment. And he that keepeth his commandments dwelleth in him, and he in him. And hereby we know that he abideth in us, by the Spirit which he hath given us* (1 John 3:19–24).

In these verses, John deals with battling doubt. He gives four directions on how true believers should respond to doubt: answer your condemning conscience before God (3:19-20), rest with confidence in God (3:21-22), exercise faith and love (3:23), and prove your sonship by the witness of the Spirit (3:24). Let's look at each of these.

## Answer Your Condemning Conscience

It is possible to be a genuine Christian and yet be unsure of one's standing in Christ. Lack of assurance can be due to many things, such as defeats in the ongoing battle with indwelling sin, the way people treat us, the accusations of Satan, or circumstances around us. When we are burdened with self-doubt, we begin asking: Am I really a Christian? Have I really believed in Jesus Christ? When I die, will I truly go into the presence of God? All of those questions can be intensified by a conscience that accuses and condemns us. No doubt many of us have been pricked in heart by thoughts such as, *How can I be a Christian? Look at what I said, look at how I behaved, look at what is running through my mind. I am at best a pathetically weak believer who has scarcely begun to live in a Christian way.* These accusations usually come in the wake of a failure in our lives or of some particularly discouraging situation in which we find ourselves. A failure in faith, in love, or in obedience prompts us to wonder, 'Am I really a Christian?' In these and many other ways, Satan is hard at work, trying to cast us into the depths of spiritual depression.

John provides helpful advice for the problem of doubt. He says, first, we are to confront our condemning consciences in the presence of our great, all-knowing God: 'And hereby we know that we are of the truth, and shall assure our hearts before him. For if our heart condemn us, God is greater than our heart, and knoweth all things' (vv. 19-20). The word *heart* here means conscience. Our conscience operates in the sphere of the conscious mind though it is rooted in the law written on the heart. How do we set our conscience, or inmost soul, at rest when it condemns us?

John highlights three things about assurance that are most welcome to the hard-pressed conscience of the child of God. First, *the accusations of should not be ignored.* The conscience is God's monitor in our souls. It reacts when sin rises. Sin has blunted the power of conscience, but conscience is still active in the human heart. It may need to be adjusted, but we should never ignore it. Those who tell us to ignore our consciences do more harm than good.

Second, *we must convinced that God's love is in us.* 'Hereby we know that we are of the truth, and shall assure our hearts before him' (v. 19). 'Hereby' refers back to what he has just said in verse 18, 'Let us not love in word, neither in tongue; but in deed and in truth.' Love for our Saviour and his people tell us that our Christianity is not counterfeit. Our walk with God may not be all it should be, but whenever our hearts condemn us, the presence of love in our hearts for the Saviour who redeemed us and for the people of God to whom we have been united, should assure our hearts of our faith before God.

When our consciences condemn us as we examine our recent thoughts, words, and actions, we should not dispute the accusations. Instead, we should point to the reality of what the Puritans called the 'in-breaking love of God' into our lives. Then we can say, 'What my heart is saying is true; I have failed and I will continue to fail until I breathe my last and have been made perfect in the presence of God. I have failed and I have fallen, but I am persuaded that God has broken into my heart and that I have become a new creature in Christ. I love his people, sinful and poor though they may be, and I love Christ before all others.'

John says we can point to actual evidence for assurance, not just things we have professed, felt, or intended. This evidence puts to rest the charges of our conscience. How easy it would be simply to say to our conscience, 'I cannot deny your accusations, but I believe in Jesus Christ; I feel stirrings towards Christ. I have made a profession of Christ.' But John speaks here of a love that is 'in deed and in truth' (v. 18). This love is willing to lay down its life for the sake of the brethren.

True Christians do not merely make a vague profession. God has replaced their heart of stone with a heart of flesh; their self-centred soul grows in manifesting the characteristics of Jesus Christ. This renewed heart looks beyond its own horizons and reaches out to embrace the people of God.

Third, to be convinced of God's love in us, *we must be convinced of God's greatness outside of ourselves.* If assurance as a Christian rested solely on my conviction of God's love in me, I would constantly fall prey to my own sins and the nagging accusations of Satan, for even my sense of that love ebbs and flows, and sometimes fails. The verdict that ultimately counts is not the one I pass on myself or that others pass on me, but the one that God passes on me. So John says, 'If our hearts condemn us, God is greater than our heart, and knoweth all things' (v. 20). John says we are to appeal, not to our consciences, but to the greatness of God as our sufficient Saviour and loving Restorer of our souls. Our hearts condemn us, but God is greater than our hearts.

To understand that appeal, read John 21, which describes how Jesus encountered Peter after his resurrection. Peter had failed Christ three times prior to the crucifixion; he even denied he knew Christ to a mere servant girl. So Jesus sought out the grieving Peter, in John 21:15–17, asking Peter three times if he loved Jesus. After the third time, Peter answered, 'Lord, thou knowest all things; thou knowest that I love thee' (v. 17). Peter knew that Christ knew the whole truth about himself, including that Peter loved his Saviour.

Peter appealed to the infinite knowledge of his Lord. He understood that our ultimate ground for quieting our consciences is not that we can point to anything in ourselves that makes us think, 'Yes, I am a Christian.' Our ultimate assurance is that we belong to the One who is rich in mercy, who does not treat us as our sins deserve. We belong to the One whose blood cleanses us from every sin.

God is greater than our hearts, greater than our sins and failures, for he is infinitely rich in mercy. He 'delights in mercy' (Micah 7:18). God's salvation exceeds our sinfulness. Here our consciences find rest.

### Rest with Confidence in God

In verses 21-22 John goes on to provide two blessings that help the believer rest with confidence in God, so that he can have a quiet conscience, void of offence. He writes in verse 21, 'Beloved, if our heart condemn us not, then have we confidence toward God.' We can have confidence before God as believers, first, because we have a *Saviour who has made atonement for all our sin.* We can take every accusation against us to the blood and righteousness of Jesus Christ, saying, 'My Saviour has paid in full the price of my sin. He has provided me with righteousness that the Father embraces. My Saviour's blood hides all my transgressions from view; therefore, my heart does not condemn me. For Christ's sake, I have confidence before God.'

A Christian approaches the eternal God with the confidence not only of a forgiven sinner but also of a restored son or daughter. Such boldness before God is not presumption. Rather, it is God's answer for our doubt. Our confidence is not based on anything we are or have done. It is centred in Jesus and what he has done. John is saying, 'Dear friends, be encouraged; we have confidence before God. We do not live in the twilight world of doubt and apprehension. We can come with confidence to the throne of God's grace because our Saviour's obedience hides all our transgressions from view.'

We also approach the Father *in* Christ. The New Testament does not normally describe the believer as a 'Christian' — the word is only used once, in Acts 13. Rather, the believer is described as someone who is 'n Christ'. Faith takes us into Jesus Christ, so that when we come to the Father we become covered by Christ. We are inseparable from Christ, for faith has brought us *into* Christ. This is why John says in verse 24, 'He that keepeth his commandments dwelleth in him, and he in him.'

Second, we also have confidence before God because *we come to him trusting that we shall receive from God anything we ask.* As verse 22a tells us, 'And whatsoever we ask, we receive of him'. John encouraged the waning spirits of believers whose confidence was undermined by false teachers by saying they would receive whatever they asked of God, if the request was in accordance with God's will.

A child is confident that he or she will be given whatever is asked of a parent, so long as the request is deemed good and right by the parent. That is precisely what Jesus teaches his disciples in Matthew 7. 'Ask, and it shall be given you', he says in verse 7. In verses 9–11, Jesus describes a son who asks his father for bread. 'What man is there of you, whom if his son ask bread, will he give him a stone? Or if he ask a fish, will he give him a serpent?' Jesus asks. 'If ye then, being evil, know how to give good gifts unto your children, how much more shall your Father which is in heaven give good things to them that ask him?'

A trusting child believes in his father's love and wisdom, and trusts his father to do what is best. A loving child does not want anything but what is good and right for him. John says in verse 22: 'Whatsoever we ask, we receive of him, because we keep his commandments, and do those things that are pleasing in his sight.' By grace, we receive of God because we show by our deeds and our desire to please him that we trust and love him and are his true children.

Obedience is doing what pleases the Father who loves us, the Saviour who redeemed us, and the Spirit who indwells us. So, no matter how we long for a prayer to be answered, whether it is for health, a job, or a relationship, the Christian concludes every prayer by saying, 'Not my will but thy will be done.' That acknowledges that we do not want to ask for anything that does not please God. We want only what he wills.

We pray that way because our heavenly Father knows what is best for us. We do not know what will happen to us today or in the future. What we think looks good to us today may have the smell of death tomorrow. Our vision is limited; we are creatures of time, not of eternity. So with a childlike love we say, 'Father, here are the desires of my heart, but grant only what pleases thee and will bring glory to thee.' Our Saviour gave us the model for prayer in the Garden of Gethsemane when he prayed, 'O my Father, if it be possible, let this cup pass from me: nevertheless not as I will, but as thou wilt' (Matt. 26:39).

**Exercise Faith and Love**

John goes on to summarize the essence of God's commands. He says in verse 23: 'And this is his commandment, That we should believe on the name of his Son Jesus Christ, and love one another, as he gave us commandment.'

Believing on Christ is the first and great commandment of the gospel. We please God when we believe in the name of his Son. The verb translated 'we should believe' is cast in the timeless (or aorist) tense. It does not refer to any particular point in time, but to a great fact — something true, fixed, and lasting. It points to the faith of one who has believed, continues to believe, and will go on believing on the name of Christ. So John is not referring simply to intellectual affirmation, which says, 'I believe Jesus is the Son of God and that he has come in the flesh.' The belief John speaks of here bows down to Jesus and embraces all that he is. True belief in Jesus means resting your entire soul upon Jesus Christ, letting him take the full weight of your sins. It means embracing him as God's Prophet, Priest, and King. It means trusting wholly in the One who has brought us God's Word, who became a sacrifice for sin, who comes to reign over us, and who defends us from every enemy. Such faith is God's antidote to doubt.

Notice how John links faith with loving one another. The commandment is to 'believe on the name of his Son Jesus Christ and love one another'. The two go together. If you do not love your fellow Christian with all your heart, then you do not believe in Christ, John says. Loving one another is the inevitable fruit of believing 'on the name of Jesus Christ'.

Does your life rest in Christ? Do you love his people? Are you exercising Christ-centred faith and obedience? If you can say yes, be assured that you are a true believer.

**Prove Your Sonship**

Knowing how fragile our hearts are, John offers in verse 24 two infallible indicators by which we can test whether we are in Christ and he in us: 'And he that keepeth his commandments dwelleth in him, and he in him. And hereby we know that he abideth in us, by the Spirit which he hath given us.' First, John says that if we keep God's commands, *our obedience shows that we now live in Christ and he in us.* By nature, we would say like Pharaoh of old, 'Who is the Lord that I should obey him?' But when we find rising within our poor hearts a new desire to please the King of heaven and a new power to do the will of God, it is a glorious indication that salvation has broken into our souls. That power may have come suddenly or gradually, but the fruit is the same: we cherish God's commandments and do them. The Spirit then nurtures that power throughout our lives, proving our sonship.

Second, *the inward witness of the Holy Spirit* also proves our sonship. John says, 'And hereby we know that he abideth in us, by the Spirit which he hath given us.' The inward witness of the Spirit goes along with a changed life. The Spirit never witnesses to our spirit apart from faith and obedience to the Father.

What, precisely, does John mean here? Does he mean that the Holy Spirit whispers some kind of assurance, telling us that we are Christians? No, John is referring here to what Paul speaks about in Romans 8:15–16 when he says to the Christians in Rome: 'For ye have not received the spirit of bondage again to fear; but ye have received the Spirit of adoption, whereby we cry, Abba, Father. The Spirit itself beareth witness with our spirit, that we are the children of God.'

The verb 'cry' that Paul uses in Romans 8 is the same verb used of Christ crying from the cross. It is the painful cry of a child of God in a moment of great need, when his whole soul is giving way. That loud, piercing cry, which came from the Saviour at the cross and which rises unbidden from the heart of the hard-pressed child of God, is God saying, 'My Spirit is witnessing with your spirit that you are my child.' That is to say, the Spirit enables us to so cry out by imparting to us the spirit of sonship, of filial love and fear. Where such attitudes are present, the Spirit is at work to produce them.

Occasionally one of our children wakes up crying in the night. The child is terrified, and cries out, 'Daddy!' We respond to that cry with an embrace that calms the fear and drives away the loneliness. That kind of response is what Jesus offered to his disciples when he told them, 'I will not leave you alone; I will send the Comforter.' He dwells in you. Your best friend will send his Spirit, who will reassure you that God is your God and you are his child.

# 16
# Testing False Prophets

*Beloved, believe not every spirit, but try the spirits whether they are of God: because many false prophets are gone out into the world. Hereby know ye the Spirit of God: Every spirit that confesseth that Jesus Christ is come in the flesh is of God: and every spirit that confesseth not that Jesus Christ is come in the flesh is not of God: and this is that spirit of antichrist, whereof ye have heard that it should come; and even now already is it in the world. Ye are of God, little children, and have overcome them: because greater is he that is in you, than he that is in the world. They are of the world: therefore speak they of the world, and the world heareth them. We are of God: he that knoweth God heareth us; he that is not of God heareth not us. Hereby know we the spirit of truth, and the spirit of error* (1 John 4:1–6).

In chapter 3, John contrasted righteousness and sin (1 John 3:4-10), love and hate (3:11–18), and faith and doubt (3:19–24). Now, in the first six verses of chapter 4, he contrasts truth and error.

## Are They Consistent with God's Word?

John has much to say about how we should think and act in a world of conflicting voices. The first counsel John gives us is that we must test the spirits. He writes, 'Beloved, believe not every spirit.' In effect he says, 'Do not be gullible; do not be mindless. Do not believe every spirit, but try the spirits whether they are of God' (4:1).

The first thing we need to know is what spirits we should test. According to John, we are to test the false prophets 'who are gone out into the world'. Technically, all who claim to be prophets today are false because the prophetical office no long-er exists. Prophets, together with apostles, were the founda-tional leaders of the church (Eph. 2:20). Prophets and apostles received direct revelation from God, which was written down for us in the Bible. The canon of Scripture is now closed. We are not to add to nor subtract from the fully authoritative, inspired, inerrant, and sufficient Word of God. Thus, anyone who claims to be a prophet today should be rejected.

Practically speaking, however, we must heed biblical warn-ings about false preachers and teachers. According to John, a preacher or teacher either speaks as the mouthpiece of the Spirit of God, heralding truth from God's Word, or speaks as the mouthpiece of the spirit of the antichrist against God.

When people claim to speak for God, our first responsibility is to examine carefully what they say and what they do. We are to be all ears and all eyes in analysing, assessing, and sifting oth-ers' words and actions on the basis of Scripture. Do not believe every spirit, John warns, for many false teachers have gone out into the world.

John wants us to ask what spirit is the moving force behind those who claim to speak on God's behalf and behind what they have to say. Is it the Spirit of God or another spirit, an un-holy, ungodly, antichristian spirit that promotes false teaching?

Too often people are taken in by false teaching, John says. They are impressed by a preacher's credentials, his mighty elo-quence, or his authoritative appearance. Such leaders must be tested to see whether their claims are true. A radio preacher or TV evangelist or popular Christian may appear to be speaking the truth, but, as Jesus warned his disciples in Luke 8:18, 'Take heed therefore how you hear'. Is what you are hearing truth or error?

Testing what others say and do to see whether it comes from God is the responsibility of every Christian, not just church leaders. As John says, 'Beloved, believe not every spirit, but try the spirits whether they are of God.'

Every believer is called to search for truth, to love truth, and to live truth without usurping the role of the church as custodian of the truth through its confessions and discipline (1 Tim. 3:15). That is to say, a discerning believer must critique from within the confessional framework and leadership of the church community. We must not act like sole arbiters of the truth. We must not react extremely to non-essential matters of faith.

The Bereans are a notable example of what it means to test the spirits. When Paul came to the city of Berea in Macedonia on his second missionary journey, the Bereans searched the Scriptures to see whether the things Paul spoke were true. They listened to what Paul said, and they tested what he said against the Word that God had spoken (Acts 17).

There are other ways to test false teachers, all of which are grounded in the Word of God. A true teacher is an influence for good and for righteousness in accord with the Word (Matt. 7: 13–20). A true teacher is orthodox in calling people to walk in the Word and the ways of God (Deut. 13). A true teacher is not motivated by financial gain (2 Cor. 2:17). A true teacher labours to bring the Saviour and sinner together by means of the Word (John 3:29). A true teacher avoids the eccentric and the bizarre so that all attention focuses on God's Word. Most importantly, a true teacher exalts Jesus Christ.

Christians are called to focus their minds on the Word, not to be impressed by a teacher's credentials or eloquence. We are to use our God-given, Spirit-informed minds to test what we hear and what we see against the Word of God.

## Do They Exalt Christ?

Second, John says that Christians must test the spirits by what they say about Jesus Christ. As John says, 'Every spirit that confesseth that Jesus Christ is come in the flesh is of God: and every spirit that confesseth not that Jesus Christ is come in the flesh is not of God' (vv. 2b–3a)

There are many ways to test teachers to see if their message is from God. One is to measure their words against what God says in the Bible. Another is to test their commitment to the body of believers (1 John 2:19), their lifestyle (3:23–24), and the fruit of their ministry (4:1). But the most important test of all, says John, is to examine what they believe about Christ. Do they affirm that Christ is fully God and fully man?

John's advice was particularly relevant for Christians of his day because of false prophets that were denying that God's Son became flesh. The prophets told believers, 'Jesus was a great man, vested with God's Spirit, but he was not God, who is pure Spirit. There is a great gulf between God and man. God would not contaminate himself with human flesh.' These prophets denied the incarnation of the Son of God in the person of Jesus of Nazareth.

For prophets such as these, John says, 'Hereby know ye the Spirit of God: Every spirit that confesseth that Jesus Christ is come in the flesh is of God' (v. 2). John is referring here to Jesus' pre-existence. Bethlehem was not where Jesus Christ began, John says. Bethlehem was where God's Son, who existed from all eternity, first appeared on earth in human flesh.

While Jesus was on earth, he said to Jewish leaders, 'Before Abraham was, I am' (John 8:58). They were furious at his claim to be God in the flesh and to have existed prior to Abraham. They looked at Jesus and said, 'You are barely thirty years old, while Abraham died two thousand years ago.'

They were wrong. As John says, 'Every spirit that confesseth that Jesus Christ is come', or has come from heaven's glory into our world, 'is of God'. Conversely, anyone who teaches that Jesus was merely a man and that he came into being in the womb of the virgin Mary has the spirit of the antichrist and is not from God (v. 3). He may be a minister, a bishop, or a professor, but he is not a true believer because the Word of God declares the pre-existent deity and glory of Jesus Christ.

Another way to test the teaching of prophets is to see if they profess that Jesus Christ has come in the flesh. The wonder of the Christian gospel is that God in all his glory is clothed in the frail, vulnerable humanity of Jesus Christ. As John 1:14 says, 'And the Word was made flesh, and dwelt among us, (and we beheld his glory, the glory as of the only begotten of the Father), full of grace and truth.'

This miracle is too mysterious to explain; we must simply bow down and accept it. God's wonders are too great to be absorbed by our fallen minds. The Incarnation of the eternal Son of God is the very truth of God.

To confess that Jesus Christ has come in the flesh is to own him as both God and man, the pre-existent yet incarnate Saviour, the all-sufficient Saviour. In his commentary, R. C. Lenski says that 'Jesus Christ is come in the flesh' summarizes the whole gospel — the entire person and ministry of Jesus. It summarizes all that John has to say in his epistle about Jesus, and all that the Scriptures have to say about Christ. It summarizes the work of all of Christ's offices. To confess Christ is to sit at his feet for prophetical instruction, to stand at his cross for bloody expiation, and to bow before his throne for royal guidance.

The spirit of the antichrist does not exalt Christ; rather, it denies the timeless truths of God and his Son. The spirit of the antichrist tries to reshape God's Son and his Word, but John is adamant that we must proclaim them as they are. John's concern here is not simply that we get our thinking right about God. John is concerned about ultimate issues; he is concerned about where people will spend eternity. John is saying, 'Do not be taken in; do not be gullible. Test the spirits; examine them carefully, because our destiny depends on how we answer the question, "What think ye of Christ?"'

## What Does the Spirit Say of Them?

We do not need to examine the spirits by ourselves; John tells us that the Holy Spirit is ready to help us, keeping us from error and guiding us into truth. As John says in verse 4, 'Ye are of God, little children, and have overcome them: because greater is he that is in you, than he that is in the world.'

By telling us that we have already overcome false spirits, John is saying that we have been and will continue to be victorious over them. We have not been hypnotized and seduced by these false spirits; we have seen through their plausible errors and overcome them. We have done that because of the One who is in us, who is greater than Satan and all of our enemies in the world.

When a Christian is regenerated, the Holy Spirit comes to dwell in him. The Spirit dwells in believers to help them glorify Christ and make them love and obey Christ. But the Spirit also comes into believers to help them discern truth from error. He does that by illuminating the Scriptures that He has written. The truth of God's Word, correctly interpreted by the guidance of the Holy Spirit, builds up a believer's faith and gives him a discerning ear.

The ability to distinguish truth from error and men of God from men of the world does not require a degree in theology or a great intellect. It requires the indwelling of the Holy Spirit and an open Bible. Combined, those two blessed gifts of God grant us a goodly measure of discernment.

When a preacher or teacher claims to speak for the Holy Spirit apart from the Scriptures, you can be sure that he knows nothing about the real ministry of the Spirit. A preacher may claim gifts of the Spirit, have much fruit on his ministry, and be popular in some circles. But great excitement, emotion, zeal, experience, and assurance, in themselves, are not sufficient proofs of the Spirit. The preacher or teacher is deluded and under the influence of a spirit of this world if he does not speak the mind of the Spirit as recorded in the Bible. As Isaiah 8:20 says, 'To the law and to the testimony: if they speak not according to this word, it is because there is no light in them.'

The Holy Spirit reacts within us when something does not tally with the Word of God. The Spirit prompts believers to question what is said and to ask, 'That does not sound right. Is that what God says in his Word?' The Spirit of truth helps us recognize error and its danger.

John tells God's children to have courage because the Lord has not left them without help: 'Ye are of God, little children, and have overcome them: because greater is he that is in you, than he that is in the world' (4:4). The Spirit of Christ is the blessed indwelling Holy Spirit, who is our Helper and Revealer. The Holy Spirit is mightier than Satan, for Satan is a fallen angel while the Holy Spirit is Almighty God.

At times, the prevalence of evil in the world and in us seems overwhelming. Evil is so strong, and we are so weak. However, John assures us that the Holy Spirit is stronger than evil and will conquer it. By God's grace, the Holy Spirit and His inspired Word live in our hearts; the Spirit opens the believer's eyes through the Word to truth. The Spirit enables believers to have their beliefs controlled by God. Such lives will bear God-glorifying fruit.

## What Are Their Fruits?

In verses 5 and 6, John contrasts false prophets with true teachers and compares the audiences who respond to each. John writes, 'They are of the world: therefore speak they of the world, and the world heareth them. We are of God: he that knoweth God heareth us; he that is not of God heareth not us. Hereby know we the spirit of truth, and the spirit of error.'

To tell a true servant of God from a false one, look at their fruits (Matt. 7:20). False servants have worldly views. Like the false prophets of the Old Testament, the lives and fruits of false prophets today are shaped by the world. They say what is popular, what pleases people, and what allows others to do what they want. Their great commandment is: 'Do whatever your heart desires.'

When God so loved the world that he gave his only Son to die, he did so to deliver sinners from their sin, not to leave them in their sin. The Gnostics, who were the false prophets of John's day, did not preach the glory of God. They did not preach the necessity of holiness. They did not preach the need for repentance. They did not preach about the awfulness of hell.

Today's false prophets are much like those of John's day. Man and his needs and his self-esteem have become the focus of everything. That is the message of the world, of false preachers and teachers. It is not the message of truth which teaches that we can only find ourselves by surrendering ourselves at the cross of Jesus Christ.

Who listened to our Lord Jesus Christ when he was here on earth? For a short time, many people listened. But John 6 says that early in Christ's earthly ministry, the crowds began to desert the teacher of truth because his sayings were too hard for them to bear.

The world listens to the lie and the error of false teachers. But, says John, 'We are of God: he that knoweth God heareth us: he that is not of God heareth not us. Hereby know we the spirit of truth, and the spirit of error' (4:6). The distinguishing mark of those who are from God is that they listen to apostolic, biblical teaching, and they obey it. As Jesus said, 'My sheep listen to my voice, and they follow me' (John 10). The unsaved are ruled by the spirit of this world. They do not listen to and obey biblical, apostolic teaching; their behaviour and conversation are dominated by worldly things. But those who are born of the Spirit and have the Spirit within them listen to us, John says, for we bring God's Word of truth. They want to know and to follow the truth. Because the Word of God is hidden in their hearts, they overcome evil and live victoriously for Jesus in this world. These are the radical differences between the Spirit of truth and the spirit of error.

We can only live for Christ if we have the Spirit of Christ in us. Paul says in Romans 8 that he who has the Spirit of Christ is the man who belongs to Christ. He who does not have the Spirit of Christ does not know Christ. Our response to God's Word tells others whether we are on the side of the world or on the side of God.

# 17

## Why We Must Love One Another

*Beloved, let us love one another: for love is of God;
and every one that loveth is born of God, and knoweth
God. He that loveth not knoweth not God; for God is
love. In this was manifested the love of God toward us,
because that God sent his only begotten Son into the
world, that we might live through him. Herein is love,
not that we loved God, but that he loved us, and sent
his Son to be the propitiation for our sins. Beloved, if
God so loved us, we ought also to love one another.
No man hath seen God at any time. If we love one another, God dwelleth in us, and his love is perfected in us*
(1 John 4:7–12).

These verses set forth the heart and glory of biblical religion.
They pulsate with life, power, and beauty. John describes the
results of Christians becoming sons of God, continuing the
theme that he has been considering since 1 John 3:1. As in
chapter 3, these verses and the remainder of chapter 4 describe
what flows out of being a true son of God: keeping God's commandments, loving one another, assurance of faith, and God
dwelling among his people, his love being revealed in them in
its fulness.

Nevertheless, 1 John 4:7 begins a new section in this epistle. Instead of contrasting the marks of sonship with the marks

of Gnostics and unbelievers, John now applies the themes he has been presenting.

Every New Testament epistle concludes with a section of application. The apostolic writers want to show us that Christianity is meant to be practiced. John, too, wants to teach us that in God's economy there is no place for teaching apart from practicing what is taught.

John begins this passage by urging believers to love one another: 'Beloved, let us love one another' (v. 7). Such love involves cherishing and valuing one another, doing good to each other as God commands, and seeking the best welfare of each other, putting their best interests above our own. All of this and much more is revealed at the cross, where Christ displays voluntary, self-sacrificial, enduring, and fruitful love that defies our understanding. That is why John goes on to say, 'Beloved, if God so loved us, we ought also to love one another' (v. 11). John is urging us to show the kind of love in our relationships with one another that indicates that we are truly God's saved and forgiven children, who have partaken of his love in Christ Jesus. John is telling us that if we do not love our fellow believers, we may be charged with being religious frauds. John says in verse 8: 'He that loveth not knoweth not God; for God is love.'

In 1 John 3:16–18, John told us that Christians are to have a self-giving, self-denying love that makes us willing to lay down its life for the good of brothers and sisters in Christ. This love is willing to empty itself for the good of the family. In 1 John 4:7–12, John gives us three reasons to motivate us to love one another. We should love one another because God is love, because God loves us, and because God's love is perfected in us.

## Where Love Comes From: Love Because God is Love

John says in verses 7 and 8 that we should love one another because God is love. He writes, 'Beloved, let us love one another: for love is of God ... He that loveth not knoweth not God; for God is love.'

The first part of John's argument for love is based on God's eternal nature. John says, 'Love one another: for love is of God.'

He adds emphatically, 'for God is love'. Love is not something that God does; it is what God is. In his eternal being and nature, God is love.

Other statements in the New Testament tell us what God is. In John 4:24, Jesus tells the Samaritan woman that God is a spirit. He is immaterial, unseen spirit. In 1 John 1:5, the apostle tells us that God is light. Light portrays that he is a God of knowledge and wisdom, and undiluted in holiness and purity. There are no shadows in God. Hebrews 12:29 tells us that God is a consuming fire. His burning holiness will either purify or consume us. So God is spirit, light, a consuming fire, and now, love.

Love and holiness are not contradictory in God. Nor do any of his other attributes conflict with love. All that God does is love because he is love. All that God does is holy and pure, because he is light. God's love is a holy love, not a blind or indulgent love. God's holiness and justice are not cold and arbitrary; they are loving holiness and loving justice.

God is a God of love. His glory is the ultimate end of all he does. God delights in himself and loves himself because he is worthy of that love. Within the Trinity, love flows between each Person of the Godhead. The Father loves the Son and the Spirit, the Son loves the Father and the Spirit, and the Spirit loves the Father and the Son (John 3:35; 14:31).

God loves his elect — those whom he chooses to save in Christ — with the same love that he has for his Son (John 17). Election has rightly been defined as God from eternity setting his love upon those whom he has chosen to save.

'God is love.' His free, sovereign, gracious love takes the initiative in loving us. God's love is the source of all Christian love. All love is of God.

John is not speaking here about mere natural, human love. When people get married, they think their love will conquer everything. They are not married long before they realize that human love has its limits. John says that we need a much deeper love. We need the love that Paul describes in 1 Corinthians 13, and that kind of love does not live in our hearts by nature. We need to draw it from a spring that can never run dry. We need to drink from the fountain of divine love if we would love one another as God intends.

John argues that because God is love, it follows that everyone who loves 'is born of God, and knoweth God' (v. 7). Conversely, 'he that loveth not knoweth not God; for God is love'. In other words, if you claim that you belong to God and know God and are part of the family of God, yet have no love for God's people, you are deluding yourself. You are trying to speak a language that is completely foreign to you.

All through this epistle, John teaches that likeness is the proof of relationship. The great proof that we are truly related to the eternal God and belong to him is that we are like him — especially in exercising love. John says that everyone who loves has been born of God. We are naturally too sinful for such divine love. Martin Luther said sin turns us in upon ourselves; we do not naturally reach out to others in selfless, self-sacrificing love. But when the Spirit of God breaks into our lives and we are 'born of God', God shows us his love for us in Christ. God plants within us the seed of a new beginning. He stirs within us a love towards those who belong to Christ.

The Bible does not allow us to rest in a merely formal relationship with God. It is possible to attend every church service and prayer meeting, to read the Bible regularly, to teach and preach the Scriptures, and yet not know God. If our lives do not manifest, even dimly, something of the love of God in Jesus Christ, then we cannot claim to be Christians.

John Owen said, 'Christian love is to be as unconfined as the beams of the sun. It doesn't select on whom it will shine its beams.' Our love should not shine only on those who we think deserve it, for who is deserving of God's love? Our love is to shine on everyone because God himself so loved the world that he sent his Son to save it. Love, as much as righteousness, is part of the Christian's birthmark. God is love, says John, so we too must extend love.

## What Love Looks Like: Love Because God Loved Us

The second reason that we should love one another, John says, is that God first loved us. In verses 9–11 we read: 'In this was manifested the love of God toward us, because God sent his only begotten Son into the world, that we might live through him. Herein is love, not that we loved God, but that he loved us, and sent his Son to be the propitiation for our sins. Beloved, if God so loved us, we ought also to love one another.'

'God *so* loved us, we ought also to love one another', John concludes. Think of that little word *so*. John is echoing his own gospel, 'God *so* loved the world'. He goes on to tell us that God's love sent his one and only Son to redeem the world. God bankrupted heaven to send us the prized Saviour; he emptied heaven of its pristine glory because he so loved us.

God sent his Son as an atoning sacrifice for our sins to bear the righteous judgement that our sins deserved (v. 10). That is why John says, 'Herein is love'. At our best and highest, at our finest and purest, we are still sinners deserving God's wrathful judgement. But he loved us. And what God has done for us is the primary incentive for us to love one another. As John Stott says, 'No one who has been to the cross and seen God's immeasurable and unmerited love displayed there can go back to a life of selfishness.'

If sin turns us in upon ourselves, the cross turns us out towards God and towards God's world. By these truths, John makes the doctrine of atonement the foundation for living in Christ. The great motivation for practical, Christ-like living is the doctrine of the cross; hence, every failure to love can be traced back to a failure to understand the cross. When the cross of Christ grips us, everything in our world changes.

'The cross is naught but love covered with flesh', wrote Samuel Rutherford. That love, says John, is manifested 'towards us'. Wonder of wonders, God loved us, who are nothing but sinners. That is the glory, the miracle, the mystery, and the beauty of the gospel.

In Romans 5 Paul tells us that God loved us — not after we reformed our lives and made ourselves better, but 'while we were yet sinners'. We only begin to appreciate the manifestation of God's love when we begin to understand the blackness, ugliness, filth, and depravity of our sin. We deserve death and hell.

Yet God has manifested his love to us! Who can comprehend the wonder of God's love toward us in Christ Jesus?

'Herein is love, not that we loved God, but that he loved us' (v. 10). Clearly God did not love us because we first loved him. By nature we hate God. We hide our faces from him. Only by grace do we love God through Christ. We love God because he first loved us.

Nothing in us and nothing we have done or might do prompts God to love us. He loves us simply because he chooses to do so. Love is his sovereign attitude toward us. He loves us, not because we are loveable, but because he is love. Our sins should repel him and move him to consign us to the lake of fire, but his love is so great that he took our condemnation and punishment upon himself. In Christ, God gave the supreme object of his love, so that he could love sacrificially to the uttermost. He gave the best he had for the worst he could find — hell-worthy sinners like us. This gracious, undeserved love motivates us to show love to others.

## How Love Grows: Love Because God's Love is Perfected in Us

Finally, John tells us, we are to love one another because God's love is made perfect in us: 'No man hath seen God at any time. If we love one another, God dwelleth in us, and his love is perfected in us' (4:12).

In the opening chapter of his gospel, John says, 'No man hath seen God at any time; the only begotten Son, which is in the bosom of the Father, he hath declared him' (John 1:18). God is the unseen God, but he has sent us his Son, who was born of a virgin and became flesh of our flesh and bone of our bone. In Christ we see the glory of God. No one has seen God, but if we love each other, we know that God lives in us.

What is more, God's love is made perfect in us — that is, it comes to ripeness, fulness, fruitfulness in us. John uses a Greek word that refers to something living that grows, matures, and bears fruit. He does not mean to say that this love is not imperfect at any point in the process.

John is saying that if we love each other, others will see God in us. They will see God's love brought to ripe fruition in us, because God has chosen to reveal his love in and through his children.

In one sense, God's love is unfinished until it radiates from his children. His love is brought to fulness 'in us', or perhaps more accurately here, 'among us'. Think of a circle. If you break the circle, it is incomplete. A completed circle is useful for many things, whereas an incomplete circle is good for nothing.

God and his children are a circle of love. If Christians do not love one another, God's love remains, in a sense, unfinished. The world looks at unloving Christians and does not see anything attractive about believing in God. What it sees is incomplete. But when the Holy Spirit prompts God's people to grow in the grace of loving one another, God's love is brought to completion.

That work of the Spirit is absolutely critical for evangelism today. In our world many people are two or three generations removed from anything Christian. Children are growing up without learning about Jesus. The Bible remains closed inside and outside of many churches. Many unconverted people do not read the Bible, and they do not sit under the preaching of God's Word. The only way they will learn about God is to see him in Christians. As Paul wrote to the Christians in Corinth, 'You are a letter, an epistle, from Christ.' People will come to know God by seeing him in those who know him, belong to him, and love him.

We must love because God is love, because God has loved us, and because God's love is perfected in us. Our love must be a compelling attraction to the lost.

# 18

## Sources of Assurance

*Hereby know we that we dwell in him, and he in us,
because he hath given us of his Spirit. And we have
seen and do testify that the Father sent the Son to be
the Saviour of the world. Whosoever shall confess that
Jesus is the Son of God, God dwelleth in him, and he
in God. And we have known and believed the love that
God hath to us. God is love; and he that dwelleth in
love dwelleth in God, and God in him. Herein is our
love made perfect, that we may have boldness in the
day of judgement: because as he is, so are we in this
world. There is no fear in love; but perfect love casteth
out fear: because fear hath torment. He that feareth
is not made perfect in love. We love him, because he
first loved us. If a man say, I love God, and hateth his
brother, he is a liar: for he that loveth not his brother
whom he hath seen, how can he love God whom he
hath not seen? And this commandment have we from
him, That he who loveth God love his brother also*
(1 John 4:13–21).

These verses tell us that God wants his children to be sure about
their relationship with him. He does not want to leave believers
in a state of uncertainty. Like every good father, God wants his
children to be assured that he loves them.

Many of God's children struggle with uncertainty. They can be so stressed by their spiritual infirmities or by life circumstances that they ask, 'How can I be sure that God lives in me, and that I am not merely deceiving myself? How can I know that God loves me?'

This, after all, is what Christianity is all about. Christianity is not simply about believing certain things; it is about the living God breaking into our lives, about 'Christ in you, the hope of glory' (Col. 1:27). As a good pastor, John picks up on the wonder that God lives in us. In these verses he gives us five ways in which we can be assured that we are God's children and that he lives in us.

## The Indwelling Presence of the Holy Spirit

How can we know that we are not counterfeit Christians? John tells us the first way: 'Hereby know we that we dwell in him, and he in us, because he hath given us of his Spirit' (1 John 4:13).

The Holy Spirit is the risen Saviour's gift to everyone who puts their trust in him. Peter promised in his great Pentecost sermon, 'Repent, and be baptized every one of you in the name of Jesus Christ for the remission of sins, and ye shall receive the gift of the Holy Ghost' (Acts 2:38).

A distinguishing mark of a true Christian is that he has received the Holy Spirit. Paul wrote to the Christians in Rome, 'If any man hath not the Spirit of Christ, he is none of his' (Rom. 8:9).

How do we know that Christ has given us his Spirit? First, we are assured of it because of the inward witness of the Holy Spirit. In Romans 8:16 Paul encourages Christians by saying, 'The Spirit itself beareth witness with our spirit, that we are the children of God.' By his mysterious, inward work, the Holy Spirit witnesses to our spirit. In effect, he tells us, 'You do fall short of living fully to God's glory as you desire, but you are no fraud; you are a child of the living God. The marks and fruits of saving grace are evident in your life.'

The true believer responds in his conscience, as it were, 'Sadly, I am not what I should be, but thanks to the indwelling presence of the Holy Spirit, I am no longer what I used to be. I cannot deny that the marks and fruits of the Spirit, which I could never produce on my own, are evident in some measure in my life. That assures me that I am a child of God.' Many Christian believers have felt that inward co-witness of reassurance between the Spirit and their own conscience.

Second, this inward witness is confirmed by the fruits of the Holy Spirit in our lives. Paul says in Galatians 5:22–23: 'But the fruit of the Spirit is love, joy, peace, long suffering, gentleness, goodness, faith, meekness, temperance'. When someone loves Christ and his people; rejoices in being a saved and forgiven sinner; has peace with God; is patient with others even as God is patient; is kind, good, faithful, and constant, then the Holy Spirit is present in that person, for these qualities are fruits of the Spirit.

It is glorious to know with certainty that the Holy Spirit dwells in us. When the struggles of life stress us and we hardly know how to deal with them, the assurance that we are by God's great mercy his own dearly loved children brings peace and stability to our soul.

## The Sureness of the Apostolic Testimony

In verse 14 John moves to a second way we are assured by the Holy Spirit: the absolute certainty of the apostles who 'have seen and do testify that the Father sent the Son to be the Saviour of the world'. The gospel is not something a few Christians have imagined; we know the gospel is true because it squares with the testimony of many others. John said in the opening verse of 1 John: 'That which was from the beginning, which we have heard, which we have seen with our eyes, which we have looked upon, and our hands have handled, of the Word of life.'

The Christian finds assurance through the eyewitness testimony of the apostles. As Peter says, 'For we have not followed cunningly devised fables, when we made known unto you the power and coming of our Lord Jesus Christ, but were eyewitnesses of his majesty' (2 Peter 1:16).

We rely upon the testimony of the apostles to Christ because it is true, not just because we feel it is true. Feelings are not an accurate gauge of truth. Feelings can deceive us. We rely on God's love because God broke into history with that love.

The Christian faith is built on the impregnable rock of what God has done, and what God has done has been written down in Holy Scripture. When we by grace put our trust in Jesus Christ, we believe the record is true about the living God's actions in time and space. We build our lives on the sure knowledge that God sent his Son into the world to save sinners. We say with John in verse 16a: 'And we have known and believed the love that God hath to us.'

The Christian anchors his assurance on the sure Word of God, which endures forever. He finds assurance when he says 'amen' to everything that God reveals about his Son through the Word, building his life on what God has spoken and done.

## The Confession of Jesus as the Son of God

The third way we find assurance is to confess that Jesus Christ is the Son of God. John says in verse 15, 'Whosoever shall confess that Jesus is the Son of God, God dwelleth in him, and he in God.' He says that God has promised to dwell in all those who trust his Son for salvation.

The confession of a true Christian that Jesus Christ is God's Son is an integral part of salvation. Paul writes, 'If thou shalt confess with thy mouth the Lord Jesus, and shalt believe in thine heart that God hath raised him from the dead, thou shalt be saved. For with the heart man believeth unto righteousness; and with the mouth confession is made unto salvation' (Rom. 10:9–10).

Mere confession of our lips is not enough. A trained parrot could say, 'Jesus is the Son of God', but the parrot would not truly believe what he said. God knows whether we truly believe what we say. True confession of Jesus Christ means being willing to stand up for him at all times, in all places, before all persons, and under all circumstances.

True confession means trusting Christ and living under his authority and lordship. It makes us willing to suffer persecution for Christ's sake. If that is true of you, then be encouraged, says John, for then you know that 'God dwelleth in you, and you in God'. God lives in you, feeble though you and your faith may be.

What a great thing it is to walk through this world knowing that though few here give you a second glance, everyone in heaven looks on with baited wonder that God, the Almighty King of glory, has chosen to live inside your frail, poor flesh.

## The Experience of God's Love

The fourth way to find assurance is to know the love of God. One day when we stand before the Lord of glory, the sure knowledge that God is love and that we have experienced that love will give us confidence and boldness. John says, 'God is love; and he that dwelleth in love dwelleth in God, and God in him. Herein is our love made perfect, that we may have bold-ness in the day of judgement: because as he is, so are we in this world. There is no fear in love; but perfect love casteth out fear' (vv. 16b–18a).

As we face God when he divides the saved from the un-saved, we will look at our lives and say, 'By grace, as Christ is, so are we in this world. We resemble him.' Being like Jesus Christ is evidence that God and his love are in you. Likeness, as we have recently seen, is proof of relationship. That is why we need not fear God on the Day of Judgement because on that day God will look at us and say, 'I recognize you; you bear the likeness of my Son. I see my love in you.'

True love casts out fear. In verse 18, John speaks of slavish fear. He uses the Greek word *phobos,* from which we derive the word *phobia.* A phobia can mean dread or terror, or it can mean awe or reverence. If you are a believer, you are com-manded to fear God, but that does not mean you must live in dread or terror of God. Rather, it means that you must rever-ence and respect God. If you are only afraid of God, something is missing in your relationship with him.

In verse 18, John tells that those who do not believe in Christ should be afraid of God and his wrath against sin because they have not been saved from their sins. Such fear involves torment, or the fear of punishment, he says.

God's people can also have fears. Some fear God's wrath, some fear witnessing for Christ, and some live in constant fear of man. These fears are needless and can be overcome. As 2 Timothy 1:7 says, 'God hath not given us the spirit of fear; but of power, and of love, and of a sound mind.' If God's Spirit dwells in us, we must not be overcome by fear. We have all the resources we need in Christ and by his Spirit to overcome fear.

'Fear is the darkroom where the devil takes you to develop your negatives', is an old saying. Fear is simply unbelief in disguise, so fear is not pleasing to the Lord. It started in Paradise when Adam and Eve listened to Satan and disobeyed God. Adam said to God in the Garden of Eden, 'I heard thy voice in the garden, and I was afraid, because I was naked; and I hid myself' (Gen. 3:10).

John says that if you are a true Christian, you should not be afraid of God. You may not be what you want to be, you may fail the Lord daily, but you need not fear. Fear has to do with punishment. Christ has borne our punishment for sin, so we have no punishment to bear. As Romans 8:1 says, 'There is therefore now no condemnation to them which are in Christ Jesus.' God's love in Christ is our assurance. That love casts out fear, for love is greater than fear. Fear prevails only when God's love is not understood and trusted.

If we know God's love experientially and trust him, we may view any afflictions that we suffer in the context of Proverbs 3:12, 'For whom the LORD loveth he correcteth; even as a father the son in whom he delighteth' (cf. Heb. 12:6). As we grow and mature in faith, we understand that God's discipline proves his love for us. It also deepens our love for him. So we must allow the truth of God's glorious love to bathe our minds daily and to wash away our fear.

'There is no fear in love; but perfect love casteth our fear: because fear hath torment. He that feareth is not made perfect in love' (v. 18). Perfect love means mature, ripened, fruit-bearing love — love that has flooded every corner of our lives and has fully persuaded us. If we continue to live in fear, we have not reached spiritual maturity. We are not allowing the love of God to take control of our minds. We are keeping God's love at a distance. We are trying to do the impossible, combining the love of a son with the fear of a slave. Mature love casts out fear. As Calvin wrote, 'The love of God, really known, tranquilizes the heart.' God's love is faithful and consistent. His love is patient and unyielding. You can count on it. That gives us encouragement and assurance.

## The Practice of God's Love

Finally, we find assurance through practicing God's love. John says in verses 20 and 21, 'If a man say, I love God, and hateth his brother, he is a liar: for he that loveth not his brother whom he hath seen, how can he love God whom he hath not seen? And this commandment have we from him, That he who loveth God love his brother also.'

John is saying that if we truly love the Lord Jesus Christ and belong to him, we will love the people of God. We will stand with them and support them (Ps. 133). If God's love is in us, it will show itself in generosity, kindness, and mercy to others.

The gospel comes to assure our hearts as well as our minds; it comes to re-centre our lives in God through his Word. The gospel does not only or even primarily come to give us fulfilment, or to make us psychologically whole, or to repair our emotions. The essence of the gospel is that we can come to Jesus Christ, be forgiven, be put right with God, and find all that our heart longs for in him.

John says, 'We love him, because he first loved us' (v. 19). Christian love is responsive. We love because God first loved us. When God's love in Christ grips us, we respond by loving other people. If we do not love other people, we truly have not experienced the love of God. Christian love is the response of a saved sinner to a gracious Saviour.

We need the assurance of knowing that the Spirit of Christ dwells in us. We need assurance in this increasingly troubled world that whatever comes, we belong to Christ. We can find that assurance through the Spirit's indwelling presence, the sureness of the apostolic testimony, the confession of Jesus as the Son of God, and the experience and practice of God's love. By means of these sources of assurance, we can stand before the judgement seat of God, not with hearts constricted by fear, but with confidence as we gaze at our Saviour and Judge upon his throne.

# 19

## Basic Truths About Faith

*Whosoever believeth that Jesus is the Christ is born of God: and every one that loveth him that begat loveth him also that is begotten of him. By this we know that we love the children of God, when we love God, and keep his commandments. For this is the love of God, that we keep his commandments: and his commandments are not grievous* (1 John 5:1–3).

John's first letter is like looking through a kaleidoscope. He keeps presenting us with the same truths, but from different perspectives. In 1 John 5, the apostle gives the kaleidoscope another turn to present a new view of the themes of loving God, loving one another, new birth, assurance, and obedience. This time, we view those themes from the perspective of our faith in Christ. John's goal in all those views remains the same: to reveal what Christianity is so that true believers will be assured of their faith and that heretics and hypocrites will be exposed for their lack of faith.

In the opening verses of 1 John 5, John shows us three truths about saving faith: what it is, where it comes from, and what it does. John's goal is to provide material so that people may examine themselves with questions such as: Is this the kind of faith that I have? Is this what I believe? Is this how faith has worked in my life? He shows us faith's nature, faith's origin, and faith's fruit.

## The Nature of Saving Faith

First, John tells us what a person of faith professes: 'Whosoever believeth that Jesus is the Christ is born of God' (5:1a). John's profession of who Jesus is and what he came to do for us and in us is clear. True Christian faith is not merely faith in faith, or 'belief in believing'. That kind of belief trusts in one's profession rather than in Christ. Such 'believism' is quite common today. Nor is it new; historically, a person who trusted in belief was sometimes referred to as a Glasite or, more commonly, a Sandemanian. Glasites are named after an eighteenth-century, Independent pastor from Scotland, John Glas (1695–1773), who trusted in belief. Sandemanians are named after Glas's son-in-law, Robert Sandeman (1718–1771), who popularized Glas's views. These men and their followers taught that a person who said he believed Jesus is Lord had saving faith. Sandemanianism reduced faith to mere intellectual assent to the truths of the gospel — assent to the proposition that Jesus saves, with no requirement of repentance, no submission to the lordship of Christ, and no experience of the power of saving truth. Sandemanianism was condemned as heresy in the eighteenth century by the church. Though only a handful of Sandemanians survive in Scotland today, believism is still popular in many evangelical circles.

But saving faith is more than a simple acknowledgement that Jesus is Lord. Jesus himself said, 'Not every one that saith unto me, Lord, Lord, shall enter into the kingdom of heaven; but he that doeth the will of my Father which is in heaven' (Matt. 7:21). Saving faith gives us spiritual vitality; it changes us and what we do. A person with saving faith demonstrates submission to the lordship of Jesus by doing the will of God.

Jesus must be Lord of our lives — not simply in word, but also in deed and truth. Genuine confession of faith is not simply belief in a belief; it is heartfelt belief in Christ as Lord. When John says, 'Whosoever believeth that Jesus is the Christ is born of God', he assumes that belief would be backed by Christ-centred living.

As the Heidelberg Catechism says, true belief is centred in Christ, the Messiah, who 'is ordained of God the Father, and anointed with the Holy Ghost, to be our chief Prophet and Teacher, who has fully revealed to us the secret counsel and will of God concerning our redemption; and to be our only High Priest, who by the one sacrifice of His body, has redeemed us, and makes continual intercession with the Father for us; and also to be our eternal King, who governs us by his word and Spirit, and who defends and preserves us in the enjoyment of that salvation he has purchased for us' (Q. 31).

Christ must be known in his Person and work. John 17:3 says, 'This is life eternal, that they might know thee the only true God, and Jesus Christ, whom thou hast sent.' This is the essence of true faith. Having this, according to John, is the first test of what it means to possess saving faith.

Today, many people not only have a mistaken notion of faith itself; they also have faith in a mistaken notion of Christ. They profess faith in a Christ of their own imagination. They conjure up the kind of Jesus that they desire rather than seeing the true Christ of the Word of God. The content of their faith is empty and meaningless. They do not have a true, experiential knowledge of the nature and content of saving faith.

## The Origin of Saving Faith

The second test of faith is its origin. Those who truly believe in Christ are 'born of God', John says. They are effectually called by the Holy Spirit which initiates new life; they are regenerated, they have the new birth, they are saved. All these expressions mean essentially the same thing: those with true faith have been transferred from Satan's realm of darkness into Christ's kingdom of marvellous light by the quickening power of the Spirit of God. Through regeneration, faith has risen in their soul. Saving faith is sure evidence that a believer has been born of God.

Some people try to illustrate faith by telling a story. 'If you are going to go from point A to point B, you get into your car', they say. 'You have faith that the car will start when you turn the ignition and that the car will get you where you want to go.

Likewise, you need to take the faith that you have and use it to believe in the promises of God.' That kind of faith is not divine faith; it is only an assumption based on probability. Because your car has run successfully so many times in the past, you have 'faith' — that is, you assume — that it will do so again. That is not the kind of faith John describes.

The faith that saves is planted in a person's heart by the Holy Spirit. A person who truly believes is born *of God*, John says. Until God opens his eyes, a person is blind to God's Son and to the truth. A person who is spiritually dead in trespasses and sins can no more exercise saving faith than a person who is physically dead can breathe. Before we can exercise saving faith, the Holy Spirit must do a quickening work in us. God must stir our hearts and enable us to believe. By his Word and Spirit, God brings faith and repentance into our lives.

## The Fruits of Saving Faith

In a final test, John now explains the fruits that saving faith produces in the life of believers. He mentions four fruits in particular, the last of which merits an additional chapter.

1. *Love for God*. Those who have been born of God love God. This response is inevitable. As John says, 'Every one that loveth him that begat loveth him also that is begotten of him' (v. 1b). When a baby is born and begins to feed upon his mother's milk, the baby grows to love the one who has begotten him. The child begins to express love to the mother. How strange it would be if God gave his life, his love, and his nature to us, and we did not return that love to him.

   Do you love God? Do you love his Word, his ordinances, his church, his salvation? We who are born of God, forgiven by God, adopted by God into the divine family, and sanctified by the Holy Spirit, cannot help but love God. Love for God is the first fruit of saving faith.

2. *Love for fellow Christians.* John goes on to say, 'Everyone that loveth him that begat loveth him also that is begotten of him. By this we know that we love the children of God when we love God' (vv. 1b–2). If we have been born of God and we love him, it is inevitable that we love others who have been born of God. When we love God, we *know* that we love the children of God because we all belong to the same family (Ps. 133).

   As members of the same family, we also think alike. When the early church met together, Scripture says, 'The multitude of them that believed were of one heart and of one soul' (Acts 4:32). The believers were of one heart and one soul because they had been born again of the same Spirit and were made partakers of the same nature.

   When we love the children of God, we express the nature that God has given to us. We share similar views, similar feelings, similar conflicts, similar interests, similar fears, and similar hopes.

3. *Obedience to God's Commandments.* When we love God, we want to obey him. As John 1:2b-3 tells us, 'By this we know that we love the children of God, when we love God, and keep his commandments. For this is the love of God, that we keep his commandments: and his commandments are not grievous.' John says that love and law belong together. We love and serve one another best by first loving and serving God. For example, a husband loves his wife best by first loving God. A mother serves her children best by first serving God. Recently, a dear believer in our congregation told me on her deathbed, 'When I was converted, I told my husband, "I still love you, but now you are in second place." I told my children that I still loved them, but I loved God most of all.' She added, 'I had a far better relationship with my husband and children after I put God first.'

Many people try to set the law of God in opposition to the love of God and true love for one another. They do not understand that to love someone truly is to cherish him as God's image bearer, to act toward him as God commands us to, and to seek what is best for him according to the will of God. If something is forbidden because it is against God's law, these people say, 'That is cold, harsh, and legalistic. We ought rather to love one another.' John refutes such thinking by saying that if we have God's nature within us and love God, we love the law of God that expresses his will and character. We love God's law just as we love everything else about God. We confess with the psalmist, 'O how love I thy law! it is my meditation all the day' (Ps. 119:97). Like Paul, we say that God's law is holy, just, and good. Like the Puritans, we speak of 'the grace of law'.

Jesus said that whoever loves God keeps his commandments (John 14:15). If we love God, we want to do as he says; we want to please him with heart, mind, and strength. We do not find his commands grievous because our soul is in the service of God. The Holy Spirit within us is our guide and helper. Too many people think of love in terms of a 'red heart'; they think of love as passion and permissiveness. According to John, love has another shape — the shape of obedience. Love is linked with obedience; we love God by obeying his commandments. As David said, 'I will run in the way of thy commandments, when thou shalt enlarge my heart' (Ps. 119:32).

God's commands are not weights that drag us down; they are wings that help us fly. We become our truest selves when we bear the yoke of Christ with joyful submission.

Does your life show that you believe this? Are you loving, joyful, and obedient to God? You might say, 'I do not keep God's commands as I ought.' Sadly, neither do I. But if you are a true Christian, failing to keep God's commands will be a great sorrow to you. You will be grieved that you do not keep God's commands as you ought and that you do not lovingly obey him as you ought. Yet the direction and intent of a true Christian's life should be unmistakable, despite its blemishes and failures. It should reflect your love and obedience to God, for you have been born anew in him. To turn to Christ involves casting off the old life of unbelief and disobedience, rooted in hating God and my neighbour, into order to take up a new life as a true believer, delighting to do what pleases him.

# 20

# *Overcoming Worldliness by Faith*

*For whatsoever is born of God overcometh the world: and this is the victory that overcometh the world, even our faith. Who is he that overcometh the world, but he that believeth that Jesus is the Son of God?* (1 John 5:4-5).

The Christian life is a struggle. It demands entrance through a narrow gate and a daily walk along a narrow path. The Christian way is not a middle way between extremes but a narrow way between precipices. It involves living by faith through self-denial, waging a holy war in the midst of a hostile world. And what a war that is, for the world doesn't fight fairly or clearly, doesn't agree to ceasefires, and doesn't sign peace treaties.

In these verses, the apostle shows how the believer overcomes worldliness by faith. Let's look at what that means, how it is practiced, and how to make it last.

## What Overcoming Worldliness Means

Earlier in his epistle, John encouraged us to flee worldliness (1 John 2:15-17). We saw at that time that worldliness is essentially human nature without God. Someone who is of this world is controlled by worldly pursuits: the quest for pleasure, profit, and position. By nature, we have a worldly mind that is 'not subject to the law of God, neither indeed can be' (Rom. 8:7).

Despite our natural worldliness, John speaks quite astonishingly of overcoming that liability. He says, 'For whatsoever is born of God overcometh the world' (5:4a). John uses that phrase sixteen times in his writings — more than all the rest of the Bible writers put together. What does he mean by 'overcoming the world'?

John does not mean conquering the people of this world, winning power battles over our colleagues, or dominating others. He is not referring to rulers such as Alexander the Great, who, after conquering the world, regretted that he had no more worlds to conquer.

Nor does John mean withdrawing from the world, such as monks or the Amish tend to do by establishing their own communities. A Christian is called to fight *in* this world even though he is not *of* this world. He must live in the world but not let the world live in him. Escaping is not overcoming. To escape from the world is like a soldier avoiding injury by running from the battlefield. Spiritual objectors have no place in the kingdom of God, for Christians are called to a war, not invited to a picnic.

For John, overcoming means fighting by faith against the flow of this present, evil world. Overcoming the world involves several things:

• *Rising above this world's thinking and habits.* Someone who wants to overcome the world realizes that he has something to overcome. He sees that he has been floating with this world's mentality — thinking the way this world thinks, speaking the way this world speaks, and spending time and energy in the pursuit of worldly things. He now realizes that his thoughts, words, and actions have all been worldly; he has done nothing to the glory of God or out of true faith in obedience to the spirit of God's law. 'I have wasted my life', he cries out. 'Rather than overcoming this world, I have been overcome by this world. Its selfishness, pride, and materialism have swallowed me up.'

• *Persevering in freedom in Christ, separate from world-ly enslavement.* Such perseverance takes great grace, for the battle against worldliness is intense. Worldly temptations and worldly people entice us. Internal worldliness afflicts us. Satan, ruler of this world, knows our weaknesses. At times, the attacks may be so powerful that we cry out with Paul, 'O wretched man that I am, who shall deliver me from the body of this death?' (Rom. 7:24). One who would overcome the world strives for allegiance to God rather than the world. Finding freedom only in Christ and his service, he cries out, 'Lord, thou hast loosed my bonds; I will fight against returning to the slavery of sin with all that is within me.'

• *Rising above the circumstances of this world.* Paul learned to be content in whatever state he found himself. Neither poverty nor wealth, sorrow nor joy could move Paul from Christ-centered living. That's what it means to overcome the world — to live, for Christ's sake, above the threats and bribes and jokes of the world. It means following the Lord like Caleb (Num. 14:24) in the midst of complainers. It means remaining at peace when friends or people at work despise us for serving the Lord. It means patiently enduring all the persecutions the world throws at us.

### Practicing the Overcoming Life

By nature, we do not possess the faith of Abraham. We are dead in our sins (Eph. 2:1-2) until God graciously makes us his own (John 3:5). Only then are we called out of this sinful world to become living members of the kingdom of God. As John tells us, 'Whatsoever is born of God overcometh the world.'

To be born of God is to be regenerated. Regeneration is that secret act of God by which he gives new life to a sinner and makes the governing disposition of his soul to be holy. Regeneration is not merely reformation, religion, or education, as Nicodemus discovered in his talk with Jesus (John 3). Rather, it is resurrection from the dead and a recreation (Eph. 2:1; 2 Cor. 4:6) that God miraculously works within us. As John Stott said,

'It is a supernatural event which takes us out of the sphere of the world where Satan rules, and into the family of God. The spell of the old life has been broken; the fascination of the world has lost its appeal.'

Those reborn of God become new creatures with radically different views of sin, the world, Christ, and Scripture. They hate sin and long to flee from it. They hate what they used to love, and love what they used to hate. They long to know Christ and to live to please him. Such people, John says, 'overcome the world'. In this respect, this overcoming is a completed and once-for-all act. Everyone born of God *has* overcome the world, John says.

Objectively, this act took place when the Son of God, lived, died, and rose from the dead, thus triumphing over sin and hell. Jesus Christ defeated Satan and the world on behalf of all those given to him by the Father from eternity. Subjectively, this act takes place in the lives of sinners who are made partakers of Christ's great act of atonement through regeneration. In John 15:19, Jesus said, 'Ye are not of the world, but I have chosen you out of the world.' Because of Christ's death, God's people have been plucked from the kingdom of this world and given to Christ and the kingdom of heaven. Through Jesus Christ, they have now overcome the world, the flesh, and the devil. We are victors not because we are great warriors, but because we belong to the One who has triumphed.

Overcoming the world is still a daily battle, however. John reminds us of that in verse 5, when he says, 'Who is he that overcometh the world, but he that believeth that Jesus is the Son of God?' Here John switches tenses to focus on how this overcoming is lived in the present. We have overcome the world because we belong to the One who has overcome, but we also must strive to win daily battles against the world.

Only faith that is rooted in Christ, is watchful, and learns to say 'no' to temptation can overcome the world. Faith gains victory over all the subtle power of worldliness by:

• *Believing in Jesus the Son of God.* John asks, 'Who is he that overcometh the world, but he that believeth that Jesus is the Son of God?' (1 John 5:5). When we become believers, our minds are enlightened, our consciences quickened, and our hearts stirred. In practice, this works through faith. By faith, we believe that Jesus is the Son of God and overcome conflict by looking away from ourselves and our weakness to his strength.

If we would overcome the world, we must look by faith to Jesus, the Son of God, who endured the cross (Heb. 12:2). The cross spelled victory for Christ, for it meant crushing the head of the serpent (Gen. 3:15) and finishing the work of suffering that His Father gave him to do (John 19:30). Jesus chose to be nailed on the cross rather than be crowned king of the world. And in those dreadful hours on the cross, the world was vanquished at his feet.

Jesus' victory on the cross was for you, dear believer. The cross is also your way to glory. When you are faced with worldly temptation, ask yourself, 'How shall I do this great wickedness against my Savior and sin against his cross?' Then confess with Paul, 'God forbid that I should glory, save in the cross of our Lord Jesus Christ, by whom the world is crucified unto me, and I unto the world' (Gal. 6:14).

You must also look to Jesus the Son of God as Almighty Intercessor and Advocate, if you would overcome the world. Everything you need in your battle against the principalities and powers of the world is to be found in Christ.

Faith obtains victory over the powers of this world because faith enables us to draw upon the resources of Christ. If you want your lamp to work, you must connect it with a power source. Likewise, faith connects us to the mighty resources of the One who has overcome the world. Those resources include Christ's merit, his life, his Spirit, and his graces.

Faith in Christ overcomes the world by making us feel at home with God and his kingdom rather than with the devil and this world. It gives us new affections through the Holy Spirit. We can truly say with Paul, 'For me to live is Christ.' Trusting in Christ alone is so simple and yet so difficult. Such faith relies utterly upon the power of his might. No wonder Matthew Henry said, 'Christ honours faith the most of all graces, because faith honours Christ the most.'

• *Purifying the heart through Christ-centredness*. First John 3:3 says that every person who has the Christian hope of being a son of God 'purifieth himself, even as he is pure'. Faith is a heavenly plant that will not flourish in impure soil. Faith is transforming. A homely person who looks at a beautiful object will remain homely, but a believer who fixes his faith on Christ is transformed into the image of Christ. Faith that looks at a bleeding Christ produces a bleeding heart; faith that looks at a holy Christ produces a holy life; faith that looks at an afflicted Christ produces sanctified affliction. And, according to Richard Cecil, 'One affliction sanctified, will do more in enabling the Christian to get a victory over the world, than twenty years of prosperity and peace.'

Faith that looks to Christ partakes of his moral excellence. By looking at Christ, the lusts of the world no longer have dominion over us. Worldliness is driven from the heart, its supreme fortress.

Christ overcame sin, Satan, death, and hell *for* us, but he also promises to be *in* us to purify us. That is the secret of overcoming the world, for, as 1 John 4:4 says, 'Greater is he that is in you, than he that is in the world.'

Satan tries to make sin attractive. Sadly, we are prone to yield to that trick. We then take sin as a sweet morsel on our tongue. But this will not happen if we put faith to work, for faith sees sin for what it is. 'Faith looks behind the curtain of sense, and sees sin before it is dressed up for the stage', wrote William Gurnall. Faith sees the ugliness of sin without its camouflage.

Of course, there will be times when the world appears to be overcoming us, times when we forget that we have conquered our worldly flesh through Christ, and we fail to live in the freedom granted us through faith. Think of the American Civil War, when the edict of emancipation freed all slaves. Long after the war was over, some freedmen went on living like slaves. Some simply could not grasp the victory that was theirs; others loved their masters and chose to wilfully serve them as bondslaves.

So it is with us Christians. We have been freed from the slavery of the world through Christ, yet we can only live like free people if we resist the attractions the world. And the only way we can do it is if we tell the world, by faith, 'All that you offer me is passing vanity. I belong to the King of kings, who has triumphed. He gives me solid joys and lasting pleasure. He has bound me to his presence and service as a willing bondslave.'

• *Living according to what pleases God.* By faith, we delight in God's delights. And, as our faith grows stronger, it increasingly tramples the world under its feet by obeying God's commandments: 'This is the love of God, that we keep his commandments ... *for* whatsoever is born of God overcometh the world' (1 John 5:3-4).

The aim of the world's commandments is to gain wealth, fame, social standing, secular power, and human pleasure. Jesus Christ aimed for none of that. He overcame the world by obeying God's commandments — loving God above all and his neighbour as himself. That is the goal of all those born of God. They yearn to obey God's commandments. And if we keep God's commandments, we will overcome the world.

We need to avoid two extremes in obeying God's commandments, however. One is legalism, which adds man-made requirements to God's commandments. The other is antinomianism, which denies the authority of the law as a rule of life for Christians. Today, our greatest problem is antinomianism. We will not be ruled by God. We fancy that our own instincts are so sanctified that we can safely follow where they lead. This thinking can lead us into the swift current of worldliness. As soon as a believer rests his oars in his battle to keep God's commandments, he yields to the world and is swept downstream, overcome by the world rather than overcoming the world in Christ.

When pleasing God becomes more important than pleasing people, the believer overcomes his love for this world's honour, riches, pleasures, entertainments, and friendships. Faith prepares him for submission in losses, self-denial, and enduring afflictions for Christ's sake.

• *Living for the unseen world that awaits us.* Faith refuses to call good evil and evil good. Faith dissolves the world's charms; it sees the world in its true colours, so that the world's control is broken. It understands that the world's best pleasures are temporary.

Faith sees there are greater pleasures to be had by abstaining from sin than by indulging in it. William Gurnall summed it well, 'The bee will not sit on a flower where no honey can be sucked — neither should a Christian.' Faith values the eternal rewards that Christ has laid up in heaven far more than all the treasures of the world (Heb. 11:25-26). In abstaining from worldly pursuits, the Christian experiences true happiness, believing that in God's presence there is 'fulness of joy' and 'pleasures for evermore' (Ps. 16:11).

## How to Make the Overcoming Last

If we overcome the world, we will be fully delivered from the world in the age to come. By faith, we believe that Christ has gone to prepare that world for us and will return to put an end to the present evil one.

By faith, we believe that the best is yet to come. We look to a time when we will be saved forever from Satan, the world, and our old nature. Sin will be left behind; evil will be walled out. There will be no more tears, pain, sorrow, temptation, or death. We will worship and praise God, serve and reign with Christ, and fellowship with the saints and angels. We will find heaven a perfect place: perfect mansions, perfect gold, perfect light, and perfect pleasure. Above all, we will be in perfect communion with the Triune God, knowing, seeing, loving, and praising him forever. Truly, 'our light affliction, which is but for a moment, worketh for us a far more exceeding and eternal weight of glory' (2 Cor. 4:17).

Overcoming the world by faith will last forever because the object of faith is the Son of God and the author of faith is the Spirit of Christ. The source of strength for the believer does not lie in himself or even in his faith in the object of that faith, Jesus, the Son of God.

All of this has much to say to us as believers in a world that seeks to trap us in its pleasures. Here are three lessons we should learn if we would persevere in overcoming the world:

• *Persevere in using the means of grace and in being a good steward of time.* A faith that does not diligently use God's means of combat is no faith at all, for it does not change us from within. When God and others cannot see a difference in our lives as we move from unbelief to faith, our faith is not real. Thomas Manton put it this way: 'A carnal Christian is no Christian but the carcase of a Christian, [for] if we don't put the love of the world to death, the world will put us to death.'

• *Repent of every backsliding way and by faith return to the Lord.* Let's heed Thomas Guthrie, 'If you find yourself loving any pleasure better than praying, any book better than the bible, any house better than the house of God, any table better than the Lord's table, any person better than Christ, any indulgence better than the hope of heaven — take alarm!' Friend, if you marry the spirit of this age, you'll find yourself a widow or widower in the age to come. Don't dress for the world to come in front of the mirror of this world. Remember, repent, return, and do the first works (Rev. 2:4-5).

• *Remember that true faith has never failed to overcome the world.* Like Christians of every generation, we grapple with besetting sins. Yet God has promised us the victory through faith! That's why faith refuses to love this present evil world. Rather, it heeds Romans 13:14, which says, 'Put ye on the Lord Jesus Christ, and make not provision for the flesh, to fulfil the lusts thereof.'

Consider the heroes of faith in Hebrews 11. They believed in God amid the worst battles of this world. They put on the; whole armour of God', especially 'the shield of faith' and 'the sword of the Spirit' (Eph. 6:10-18). So should we. Jesus said, 'Be faithful unto death, and I will give you a crown of life.'

# God's Testimony of His Son

*This is he that came by water and blood, even Jesus
Christ; not by water only, but by water and blood. And
it is the Spirit that beareth witness, because the Spirit is
truth. For there are three that bear record in heaven, the
Father, the Word, and the Holy Ghost: and these three
are one. And there are three that bear witness in earth,
the Spirit, and the water, and the blood: and these three
agree in one. If we receive the witness of men, the witness of God is greater: for this is the witness of God
which he hath testified of his Son. He that believeth
on the Son of God hath the witness in himself: he that
believeth not God hath made him a liar; because he
believeth not the record that God gave of his Son. And
this is the record, that God hath given to us eternal life,
and this life is in his Son. He that hath the Son hath
life; and he that hath not the Son of God hath not life*
(1 John 5:6–12).

John declares in 1 John 5:5 that Jesus is the Son of God. For
evidence supporting this truth, John could have presented
the eyewitness accounts of himself and others who had seen
Jesus in person, as he did in the opening verses of this epistle.
Human testimony is important. Without it, justice would hardly
be possible in this world. To prove the guilt or innocence of an

individual in a court of law, witnesses come forward and give testimony, which is used as evidence in the case. God sanctioned the acceptance of human testimony under Old Testament law. Deuteronomy 19:15 says, 'On the evidence of two witnesses, or of three witnesses, shall a charge be sustained.' John affirms that in verse 9, saying 'we receive the witness of men'.

Far greater than the witness of men is the witness of God: 'If we receive the witness of men, the witness of God is greater: for this is the witness of God which he hath testified of his Son' (1 John 5:9). Some people testify that Jesus is the Son of God while others testify that he is not. So the witness of man is not enough. However, if God himself appeared on the witness stand, stating whether or not Jesus is his Son, that would settle the matter, because God is always truthful; he 'cannot lie' (Tit. 1:2).

## Witnesses in Heaven and on Earth

We do not have to call God to the witness stand, for he has already 'borne witness concerning his Son', John says. The word *witness* is used nine times in 1 John 5:6–12. It comes from the Greek word *martureo*, which means, 'one who remembers or who has knowledge of something by personal experience'. The word describes those who give testimony in a legal matter.

In 1 John 5:7–8, the apostle mentions three witnesses God has given in heaven and three on earth to confirm that Jesus is indeed his Son. Verse 7 has become known to students of the Greek New Testament as the 'Johannine Comma' — *comma* being used in its technical sense as a short group of words contained in a treatise or argument. Verse 7 is a section of John's argument concerning the Triune God's witness to his incarnate Son. Many scholars have concluded that this verse is a later addition to the Bible, since it is not included in most ancient Greek manuscripts. Others have defended the possibility that this verse is an authentic part of the original text of First John (see Edward F. Hills, 'The Johannine Comma', *The King James Version Defended*, pp.209-213). To enter that debate here, however, would take us too far afield from the argument John is presenting.

The truths expressed in this verse cannot be denied, however. The Old Testament teaches the unity or 'oneness' of God, declaring that God is one indivisible substance (Deut. 6:4). The New Testament teaches that there is a trinity or 'threeness' of Persons in the Godhead, the Father, the Son, and the Holy Spirit (Matt. 28:19; 2 Cor. 13:14; Eph. 1:1-14). The Christian church confesses 'that we worship one God in Trinity, and Trinity in Unity; neither confounding the Persons nor dividing the substance' (Athanasian Creed, Articles 3 and 4).

The Father bore witness to Christ in his decree, saying, 'Thou art my Son' (Ps. 2:7-9; cf. Ps. 89:19-29); at Christ's baptism, saying from heaven, 'This is my beloved Son in whom I am well pleased' (Matt. 3:17); in answering Christ's prayer by works of power (John 11:41); and by raising him from the dead (Rom. 1:4). Christ bore witness to himself by word and deed, confessing and showing himself to be the incarnate Word and Son of God. The Holy Spirit bore witness to the Son before his advent, speaking by the prophets; during his ministry on earth, descending and remaining upon him as an anointing from God; and after his ascension into heaven, in the preaching and acts of the apostles and the life of the growing church. We have ample grounds to believe that 'there are three that bear record in heaven, the Father, the Word, and the Holy Ghost: and these three are one'.

In verse 8, John speaks of witnesses on the earth: 'There are three that bear witness in earth, the spirit and the water and the blood: and these three agree in one.' God's witness is enough by itself, but in order to fully convince us, John brings forth three earthly witnesses. Actually, these witnesses are three aspects of the one witness of God. Unlike the false witnesses that accused Jesus when he appeared before the Jewish Sanhedrin, these witnesses are in agreement. As John tells us in verse 9, all three of God's witnesses agree in affirming Christ as the Son of God.

**The Witness of Water**

Verse 6 says that Christ 'came by water and blood'. This phrase
has been explained in various ways. Augustine and several
recent writers believed the verse refers to John 19:34, which
states that a spear was thrust into Jesus' side, bringing forth
'blood and water'. However, this view does not coincide with
John's purpose of challenging the heretics who believed that
Jesus came by water but not by blood (see v. 6). Others, including Luther and Calvin, believed these words refer to the
sacraments: the water of baptism and the blood of the Lord's
Supper. But that view also misses John's emphasis on Christ's
historic incarnation. The majority of interpreters today rightly
see water and blood as summing up the incarnational work of
Jesus Christ here on earth, beginning with his baptism by water
and culminating in his crucifixion by blood.

John says that Jesus 'came', indicating the historical fact
of his coming into the world as the promised Messiah. Jesus
entered his office as Messiah by water; he was baptized by John
the Baptist 'to fulfil all righteousness' (Matt. 3:15). When Jesus was baptized, he was fulfilling Numbers 8:6–7, which shows
that the Levites were ceremonially cleansed by the sprinkling of
water as they were ordained into the priesthood. Jesus Christ,
our eternal High Priest, was baptized as the ceremonial act of
his ordination to the priesthood.

The water of baptism was a witness that Jesus was truly
the Messiah. At Jesus' baptism, the Holy Spirit descended upon
Jesus like a dove (Matt. 3:16), signifying that in his baptism,
Christ was also anointed with the Holy Spirit. The voice of God
the Father from heaven also testified that Christ was the Son of
God (v. 17).

**The Witness of Blood**

Jesus came by blood as well as water, John says in verse 6. The
Gnostics taught that the Christ came upon Jesus at his baptism
but left him prior to his death. The Son of God could not die,

the Gnostics said, for death is a sign of weakness. To counteract that false teaching, John stresses that Jesus Christ came not
only by water, but also by blood, that is, by the cross.

Christ suffered and bled and died upon the cross. In Luke
24:26–27, Jesus said to the two disciples on the road to Emmaus, 'Ought not Christ to have suffered these things, and to
enter into his glory?' Jesus then taught them all the scriptures
from Moses and the prophets explaining who he was. The cross
was proof that Jesus was the Christ, for the prophets had said
that Christ would suffer and pay the penalty for the sins of his
people (Isa. 53).

Several factors are involved in the witness of the blood. First,
Jesus' death on the cross fulfilled prophecy, which said that the
Messiah would suffer and die. Second, the Father testified with
various signs that Jesus was the Christ on the cross: he turned
midday into midnight, rent the temple veil, sent an earthquake,
opened tombs, and raised dead believers to life. Finally, Christ's
resurrection from the dead testified that Jesus was the Son of
God incarnate (1 Cor. 15:3-4).

The Gnostics were doing precisely what heretics do today
and have done in every day: they rationalized the gospel. They
tried to bring the gospel down to where it fit comfortably into
human thinking. Today, heresy takes a different form. Instead
of denying the humanity and suffering of Christ, today's heretics deny all that is supernatural. They deny the Virgin Birth of
Christ, finding it too hard to believe. They cut out the Incarnation, asking, 'How could God become man? It is impossible
according to *my* mind.' As for the miracles of Christ, they say,
'How can we believe in them? They are just stories concocted
to impress gullible people.' They remove all that people find
hard to believe and construct a Christian faith that is devoid of
anything divine.

Christians of every age are called to battle for the truth of
Jesus Christ. If Jesus Christ was not God and man, his death on
the cross for sinners is meaningless, devoid of power and significance. The cross is meaningful only because of who died on
it. No one but God could deal with the awful penalty of sin. The
Bible becomes meaningless if Christ was not the Son of God.

We must begin with Christ when we speak with unbelievers. When Saul of Tarsus was gloriously converted on the road to Damascus, the first thing he did was go into the streets of Damascus — not to talk about himself or his experiences, but to preach Jesus Christ, who came by water and blood.

Faith builds on the truth. That is why people have to be confronted with the undeniable, historical truth of what God has done in history in his Son, Jesus Christ. Otherwise, people will respond by saying, 'Christianity may suit your taste but it does not suit mine.' John teaches us that the gospel does not cater to people's tastes; it confronts people with the truth. Heaven and earth witness to that truth.

## The Witness of the Spirit

The third witness to the truth about Christ Jesus is the Spirit: 'And it is the Spirit that beareth witness, because the Spirit is truth' (v. 6). The Holy Spirit can be fully trusted as a witness because he is truth itself, John says. Since the Spirit is God, he cannot speak anything other than the truth. Jesus said, 'When the Comforter is come, whom I will send to you from the Father, even the Spirit of truth, which proceedeth from the Father, he shall testify of me' (John 15:26).

The Holy Spirit testifies through the water and the blood. He testified at the baptism of Christ, at the cross, and in raising Christ from the dead. But in John 15:26, Jesus speaks of the testimony of the Spirit after the ascension. He refers to the work of the Holy Spirit from Pentecost onward. Acts 5:30-32 also refers to this witness of the Spirit, when Peter says, 'The God of our fathers raised up Jesus, whom ye slew and hanged on a tree. Him hath God exalted with his right hand to be a Prince and a Saviour, for to give repentance to Israel, and forgiveness of sins. And we are his witnesses of these things, and so is also the Holy Ghost, whom God hath given to them that obey him.'

The Holy Spirit testified that Jesus was the Son of God and only Saviour of the world through the preaching of the apostles and the confirmation of their preaching by signs, wonders, and miracles. The Spirit testified by converting millions of souls since the day of Pentecost, and still testifies today as the Scriptures are faithfully proclaimed, convicting and persuading those who listen that Jesus is the Son of God, Saviour and Lord. The Spirit testifies through the Word of God. As the Westminster Confession of Faith says: 'Our full persuasion and assurance of the infallible truth and divine authority (of the Bible), is from the inward work of the Holy Spirit bearing witness by and with the Word in our hearts' (1.5).

By revealing the Holy Spirit as the third witness on the earth, John recognizes that alongside the objective historical facts of Jesus Christ's life and death, there is the inward, persuading ministry of the Holy Spirit. He writes of the Spirit in the present tense, as if to say, 'It is the Spirit that beareth witness, and he keeps on testifying to us.'

If someone asked, 'Why are you a Christian?' I could give one of two answers. The first would be: 'I am a Christian because what the Bible tells me is true.' The second, more profound answer would be: 'Because the Holy Spirit has opened my eyes to see Jesus Christ as the Son of God, to believe it, to love it, and to build my life on it.' The second response is what John stresses here. It is one thing to acknowledge facts; it is another thing to embrace the truth that the facts proclaim.

Some people do not like facts; they run away from them. They cannot deny the facts of God's Word, but they don't allow those facts to affect their lives. The Holy Spirit makes facts come to life so that when we read and listen to God's Word, we hear not only words, but truth that pulsates in our hearts. The Spirit makes us feel the power of the truth and gives us the desire to yield to the force of truth. As Calvin says, 'It is the Holy Spirit who seals in our hearts the testimony of the water and the blood.'

Christianity is a supernatural faith. Yes, we have proofs of its validity — we bring people facts that appeal to their minds. But unless the Holy Spirit, the great Persuader, opens a person's heart, he will never know the truth. Paul told the Corinthians, the 'natural man receiveth not the things of the Spirit of God: for they are foolishness unto him: neither can he know them, because they are spiritually discerned' (1 Cor. 2:14). He went on to say, 'No man can say that Jesus is Lord, but by the Holy Ghost' (1 Cor. 12:3). Sin so blinds us that we cannot see the truth. That is why people who have been taught the Bible can miss the truth within it. But when the Spirit testifies inside us, he awakens us to the truth, and we understand the Scriptures as never before.

John says in verse 10, 'He that believeth on the Son of God hath the witness in himself.' The Spirit witnesses in his soul the truth of Scripture's teachings. The true believer falls in love with the Bible because it unveils Jesus Christ, who becomes the peace of his heart, the love of his life, the source of his energy, the theme of his song. What a blessing to believe God's testimony about his Son and to have the Spirit of God authenticate that faith within us by the Word!

This witness of the Spirit keeps growing as the believer's life experience underscores God's testimony of his Son. To illustrate, suppose you are an employer looking for a new employee. You interview one candidate who presents you with an excellent resume. The interview goes well. But until you actually have that person working for you, you cannot be sure about how that person will perform. There could be flaws in a person's character or work habits that were missing from the resume or not apparent in the interview.

Now suppose that you hire this person and after a few months, you realize how much he exceeds your expectations. Your employee is better than what was stated on his resume. You experience such great satisfaction with your choice that you can only extol your new employee's abilities.

Similarly, the person who believes God's witness of his Son experiences more and more how true that witness is. Christ exceeds our greatest expectations. He offers — and delivers — more than we could possibly expect as we grow in understanding and experiencing repentance, faith, justification, sanctification, adoption, perseverance, and assurance. The believer finds Christ so altogether lovely that he can only respond, 'As the years go by and I compare what Christ has been to me with what God says about Christ in the Bible, I find that the promises are all true. Christ is even better than what can be put into words. My conscience witnesses that he is mine and I am his.'

This internal witness enables believers, in turn, to be witnesses for God. As Jesus said, 'He [the Holy Spirit] shall testify of me: and ye also shall bear witness' (John 15:26–27). God will use your witness to reach lost sinners. Ask God to help you proclaim the truth of his Word and to be a powerful witness of his amazing Son.

## Calling God a Liar

In addition to the trustworthy witnesses of water, blood, and Spirit, John stresses one more reason for believing God's testimony: 'He that believeth not God hath made him a liar; because he believeth not the record that God gave of his Son' (v. 10). When we do not surrender to the truth about Christ, we claim to know the truth more than God does. We do not dare to literally say God is a liar, of course, but that is the position we take in refusing to bow to the truth of God's testimony of his Son.

If we reject God's testimony, we will remain under God's awful judgement. Making a liar of God is the most foolish thing a person could do, for it rejects the salvation God that has provided. It insults God. Yet this is exactly what every person does by nature, for we do not naturally believe the record God gives of his Son. Unbelief is not a misfortune to be pitied; it is a sin to be deplored. John says that if we do not embrace the revelation that God has given, we are saying with our lives: 'God is a liar. I cannot believe him. I will not yield my life to his Son.'

God confirms the truth about his Son through trustworthy witnesses. The evidence is irrefutable that Jesus is Lord of all, the second member of the Trinity.

## The Consequences of This Testimony

John concludes that those who believe in God's Son will have life, and those who do not believe will not have life (vv. 11-12). God gives us eternal life when we embrace his testimony about his Son. John 17:3 says, 'And this is life eternal, that they might know thee the only true God, and Jesus Christ, whom thou hast sent.'

Do you ever stop and think: 'Well, I am alive. My heart is beating, my pulse races, my eyes blink, my feet move. What does he mean, "that ye might have life"'? Because of sin, we are dead by nature. Sin has deadened us to God. Christ came to make us alive, to bring us back to our Creator, who is our Father. This fits John's recurring theme: Life that is truly life is life lived in fellowship with God.

In effect, John is saying: 'Be encouraged, no matter what unbelievers say to you to knock you off course. If you have Jesus Christ, the Son of God, you have life. You have the one thing that ultimately matters — fellowship with God.'

Those who do not believe Christ is the Son of God do not have life (v. 12b). To turn from God's testimony of his Son is to spurn the mercy and love of God himself and life eternal.

How would you feel if you walked down Main Street today and saw nothing but walking skeletons? Your mind and heart would recoil at the grotesqueness. Yet that is what God sees when he looks at people who do not have Jesus Christ — spiritual skeletons. People without Jesus are spiritually dead.

John wants us to understand how serious unbelief is. We hear much about cancers, heart attacks, strokes, AIDS, and other life-threatening diseases. Our heart goes out to people with such diseases. But there is something infinitely worse than contracting AIDS or cancer. Unbelief will kill you spiritually and send you to a godless eternity.

What do we do with that restless ache within us that hankers after real life? We may be like the people Herman Bavinck wrote about when he said: 'They seek God down below and he is up above. They seek him on the earth, and he is in heaven. They seek him in money, property, fame, power, and in passion, and he is found in the high and holy places, and with him who is of a contrite and humble spirit. They seek him, and at the same time flee from him.'

'Man longs for truth and is false by nature', Bavinck went on. 'He yearns for rest, and throws himself from one diversion upon another. He pants for a permanent and eternal bliss, and seizes on the pleasures of a moment. He seeks for God and loses himself in the creature. He is a born son of the house, and he feeds on the husks of the swine in a strange land. He is as a hungry man who dreams he is eating, and when he awakes, finds that his soul is empty. Science cannot explain this contradiction in man. Man is an enigma whose solution can be found only in God.'

As a hymn-writer put it:

*For none but Christ can satisfy,*
*None other name than he.*
*There is love and life, and lasting joy,*
*Lord Jesus, found in thee.*

# 22

# *How to Grow in Assurance*

*These things have I written unto you that believe on the name of the Son of God; that ye may know that ye have eternal life, and that ye may believe on the name of the Son of God. And this is the confidence that we have in him, that, if we ask any thing according to his will, he heareth us: and if we know that he hear us, whatsoever we ask, we know that we have the petitions that we desired of him. If a man see his brother sin a sin which is not unto death, he shall ask, and he shall give him life for them that sin not unto death. There is a sin unto death: I do not say that he shall pray for it. We know that whosoever is born of God sinneth not; but he that is begotten of God keepeth himself, and that wicked one toucheth him not. And we know that we are of God, and the whole world lieth in wickedness. And we know that the Son of God is come, and hath given us an understanding, that we may know him that is true, and we are in him that is true, even in his Son Jesus Christ. This is the true God, and eternal life. Little children, keep yourselves from idols. Amen (1 John 5:13–21).*

John wrote his first epistle to show believers how to increase in their fellowship with the Father, the Son, the apostles, and the saints. He concludes his first epistle by reminding readers that he also wrote to help them grow in assurance of faith: 'These things have I written unto you that believe on the name of the Son of God; that ye may know that ye have eternal life, and that ye may believe on the name of the Son of God' (5:13).

John writes as a caring pastor to believers whom he knows so well that he fondly calls them 'little children'. He writes to assure them of their standing in Christ. God wants them to be sure that they are truly his, for God does not want his children to live in uncertainty.

Some people ask, 'How can anyone be sure of eternal life? Is it not presumptuous to be assured?' Yes, carnal presumption is a real possibility. Many people in John's day as well as in ours claim assurance even though their lives do not support that claim. But John is speaking here of genuine assurance, not carnal presumption.

Those who have real assurance yearn to grow in assurance to the glory of their Saviour and Lord. Growing in assurance is critical for a healthy spiritual life. If you have wondered how to obtain assurance, how to keep it, and how to persevere in it, John offers several directives in the concluding verses of his first epistle.

## Assurance through Prayer

The first directive explains the role of prayer. In verses 14-17, John describes prayer as a means of grace through which the believer can grow in unbounded assurance. He writes, 'And this is the confidence that we have in him, that, if we ask any thing according to his will, he heareth us: and if we know that he hear us, whatsoever we ask, we know that we have the petitions that we desired of him' (5:14-15).

The point John makes here is that praying with confidence is grounded in an assured relationship with God. It is grounded not simply in the relationship of a creature to his Creator, or even of a sinner to his Saviour, but in the relationship of a child to his Father. This relationship gives us the assurance to come to God with boldness, knowing that we can ask anything according to his will, and he will hear us (v. 14).

Prayer is not merely a convenient device for imposing our will on God or of bending God's will to our will. Prayer is God's method of subordinating our will to his will and to Christ's lordship. John reminds us here that the heart of confident prayer is that if we ask anything 'according to his will', God hears us.

The mature Christian wants nothing beyond the good, acceptable, and perfect will of God. Knowing that the Father loves him and that he belongs to God, the Christian believes that God will withhold no good thing from him. That is why at the heart of every mature Christian prayer is the longing, 'Not my will but thy will be done.'

Let us learn the blessedness of bending our will to God's, discovering in the process how he withholds no good thing from his children. Jesus said, 'If ye then, being evil, know how to give good gifts unto your children, how much more shall your Father which is in heaven give good things to them that ask him?' (Matt. 7:11). What assurance that brings us! We not only know that we belong to God but that God wants to bless us with goodness all the days of our lives.

## Interceding for a Brother Who Sins

John goes on to show how a Christian's confidence can grow through intercessory prayer for professing Christians who have sinned. He writes, 'If a man see his brother sin a sin which is not unto death, he shall ask' — that is, he should pray with assurance in accord with God's will — 'and he shall give him life for them that sin not unto death. There is a sin unto death: I do not say that he shall pray for it' (vv. 16-17).

John is talking about two kinds of people in this passage: one who sins but not unto death and one whose sin is unto death. Neither person is behaving like a brother. Earlier, John wrote about those who 'have gone out from us' (2:19). True believers want the best for each other, so if someone stumbles and falls, our hearts do not want to relinquish the possibility that the 'brother' is a true Christian. He may not be a true believer, but we are deeply grieved at that prospect. He was once a part of us but now is outside the church and outside the fellowship.

The first type of person John refers to in verse 16 is the vast majority of people who have not sinned the sin unto death. They have not blasphemed against the faith. These people are backsliding and becoming more worldly, and, in most cases, have lost the joy and peace of believing. Yet they are not completely lost, so John urges us to pray for them. God may answer those prayers by granting them new life, either through renewal or first-time belief. Because the Father's will is that none of his children should perish, we can pray with confidence, 'Lord, restore him, renew him, bring him back.'

This is where true mutual watch and caring for one another begins. If we see a brother or sister commit a sin, we should not gossip about it, saying to others: 'Have you heard about so and so?' Rather, we speak privately, and in love, to the offending brother and sister, following the directions set forth by Jesus in Matthew 18:15–17. Most importantly, we pray for the brother or sister. We bring that person and his situation to the Lord, for God promises to grant life when we do that. How humbling and assuring to realize that we can become the channels of prayers through which God will transform the lives and hearts of backsliding sinners!

John then addresses the more difficult case of those who have sinned 'unto death' — that is, who have sinned beyond any reasonable hope of repentance and restoration. In the context of verse 13 and the rest of the epistle, the sin that leads to death is apparently the sin of the false teachers who were causing great distress to Christians by teaching that Jesus was not God's incarnate Son. These teachers denied that salvation was to be found in Christ alone. In so doing, they departed completely from the faith, rejected everything they once believed in, and blasphemed the Lord and his servants and people. They were moving dangerously close to committing the sin which leads to eternal death, the so-called 'unpardonable sin'. By blatantly denying Christ, they were sentencing themselves to death.

Commentators are divided on what John means in saying, 'I do not say that he shall pray for it.' Is John saying that we should not pray for people who have left the fellowship of believers? Some emphasize that this passage could also be translated from the Greek: 'I do not say that you should inquire about that', meaning that people should not try to figure out who has committed the sin unto death. Practically speaking, it is very difficult to determine who has committed this sin, and therefore we should, as a general rule, persevere in prayer for every person, remembering that it is better to err on the side of charity than judgement.

What John appears to be saying here is that even if you were to pray for someone who, in the language of Hebrews 6, has crucified the Son of God afresh, has tasted of the heavenly gift, and has trampled on the blood of Christ, you cannot be confident that God will restore such a person in response to intercessory prayer. While John stops short of forbidding us to pray for such people, he withholds any expectation that God will answer such prayers. John does not want to raise false hopes. But you *can* be confident that God will restore someone who commits a sin that is not unto death and has not publicly trampled on the blood of Christ.

The truth that ought to impress us here is the awful state of people who publicly reject the gospel and trample on the blood of Christ. Verse 16 tells us it is possible to deny Christ beyond the point of salvation. It speaks of people who have so hardened their hearts against God that God now allows them to reap the everlasting consequences of walking out on the Son of God. How deadly sin is!

There is a close connection between growing in assurance and persevering in intercessory prayer. As God answers your prayers, does this not help you become more assured and more persistent in your faith? Oh, that we would pray with Thomas Chalmers, leader of the 1843 Disruption in Scotland, who once wrote in his diary: 'Make me sensible of real answers to actual requests, as evidences of an interchange between myself on earth and my Saviour in heaven.'

The greatest blessing of intercessory prayer is that you bring glory to God when you pray for others. God wants you involved in the lives of others through intercessory prayer. Are you praying for your backsliding or unconverted brother and sister? Are you praying for those who are becoming more worldly and for those who are persisting in sin?

## Building Assurance on the Certainties of the Christian Life

John goes on in verses 18–20 to tell us how to grow in assurance. Note how the opening words of all three verses are 'we know'. John wants Christians to grow in assurance by leaving them with three unassailable certainties at the end of his letter:

1. *Victory over sin.* Verse 18 says, 'We know that whosoever is born of God sinneth not.' John has already expressed this idea in 1 John 3:9. Now he reminds his readers to persevere in their battle against sin in order to have greater measures of assurance. To summarize, John is saying that the one who has been born of the Spirit does not continue in a lifestyle of sin; he does not persist in sin.

   With new birth or regeneration, a new heart and spiritual life are implanted in an individual. The lifestyle of the believer changes from darkness to light. The believer cannot change back into an unregenerate person who is dead in sin; God's seed, that is, God's life, remains in the believer. Therefore he does not abide in sin, indeed, he cannot. Persisting or living in sin is incompatible with being a child of God.

   If you have been born again, you no longer have to yield to your sinful desires. You have all the resources you need in the Triune God to claim victory over the evil within you, which the Bible calls the flesh. By God's grace, you can overcome your sinful desires and obey his commandments.

   In verse 18, John says, 'He that is begotten of God keepeth himself.' Most manuscripts do not include the word 'self', so many translations only say that Christ keeps those begotten of God. There is, of course, much

scriptural support for Christ being the keeper of his flock
(cf. John 17). On the other hand, Scripture holds firm
the concept of a Christian keeping himself. First Timothy 5:22 speaks of believers keeping themselves pure,
James 1:27 of keeping themselves unspotted from the
world, and Jude 21 of keeping themselves in the love
of God. Altogether, Scripture is quite plain: Behind our
efforts to keep ourselves stands the work of Christ and
the Holy Spirit.

If you are a believer, you know that if left to yourself,
you would fall away, but because you are kept by the
Son of God, you will never turn your back on God or
go back permanently to your former way of life. You
'are kept by the power of God through faith unto salvation' (1 Peter 1:5). Paul summarized it well in Philippians 2:12–13, 'Work out your own salvation with fear
and trembling, for it is God which worketh in you both
to will and to do of his good pleasure.'

The saints persevere because the Saviour preserves,
protects, and keeps them. As 2 Thessalonians 3:3 says,
'The Lord is faithful, who shall stablish you, and keep
you from evil.' Dear believer, the Lord Jesus Christ is
still interceding for you at the right hand of the Father.
If Christ is praying that you will not be overtaken by the
evil one, then be assured, as John 17:15 says, that his
prayers for you will be answered and that, as 1 John
5:18 says, the wicked one will not touch you.

'Wait a minute', you say. 'I thought we were in a
battle with the devil, and he roams around seeking to
devour us.' Yes, we are at war with Satan and his min-
ions. Yes, he would like to devour you, but he cannot
— if you are in Christ.

If you are in Christ, the devil cannot take you back
into his grip. The Greek word for 'touch' in this verse
means 'to fasten one's self to, adhere to, cling to'. The
only other time John uses this word is in John 20:17,
when Jesus appeared to Mary Magdalene after the resurrection and said to her, 'Touch me not; for I am not

yet ascended to my Father.' If you are a believer, you
are no longer in the clutches of the evil one. Satan cannot take away your salvation, he cannot possess you,
and he cannot seriously harm or injure you or make
you sin.

Having said that, the devil is still a formidable enemy. As Martin Luther wrote, 'His craft and power are
great.' The devil can still tempt and try you. John Bunyan said, 'When one trial doth me leave, Another trial
doth me seize.' If you are not aware of Satan's schemes,
you will fall for them. If you are not keeping watch and
praying, the devil will entice you to sin. But the devil
cannot make you sin without your cooperation. He cannot control you from within but must work through out-
ward means. Satan works through the world to appeal
to your fleshly desires. If you yield to his temptations,
you are responsible, not the devil. But as you look to the
Lord Jesus, he will protect you from the temptations of
the evil one. We *know* that we have victory over sin and
Satan because Christ is our keeper.

2. *Belonging to God.* John says in verse 19: 'We know
   that we are of God, and the whole world lieth in wickedness.' So if you have been born of God, you belong
   to God. At one time you were in the world and under
   the sway of the wicked one. But now you belong to the
   Lord. You have a different Father, God; a new Master,
   the Lord Jesus Christ; a different influence, the Holy
   Spirit; and a new standard, the Word of God. You belong to a new family, the church of God, and you live
   with a new purpose, the glory of God. Since you now
   belong to God, you must live like it. You must not live
   like those in the world because you are no longer of the
   world.

   Here John contrasts believers with unbelievers. We
   who believe in the Lord Jesus Christ are 'of God'. Unbelievers are under the sway or influence of the wicked
   one. Being 'of God' means that God is the source of

your spiritual life and being. You lie in his embrace because you belong to him by covenant.

'We know that we are of God, and the whole world lieth in wickedness', John says. Christians know who they are and what the world is. Christians know that sin is not an occasional blemish but a mark of Satan's rule in people's lives. We know, by grace, that we are children of God, while millions in the world are under the influence of the evil one.

So many people think they are free, yet they are in bondage to the prince of darkness. But the gospel opens our eyes to know who we are in ourselves and who we are in Christ, and then we confess gloriously, 'I am his and he is mine.' We look at this world with all its attractions and see it as shallow and empty. If you belong to God by faith in Jesus Christ, then take care that you do not live as those who belong to the world. Live like a child of God, separated from the world and dedicated to holiness. That does not mean you have no interaction with people in the world, but you and I must not be conformed to the pattern of this world. Instead, we must become more like the Lord Jesus. We must become imitators of God, our heavenly Father — because 'we know' we are of God.

3. *Knowing the true God.* John says in verse 20: 'And we know that the Son of God is come, and hath given us an understanding, that we may know him that is true.' The Christian faith is grounded in truth. We know that the Incarnation was real. The Son of God has come and has given us understanding. The Christian life begins with the renewal of our understanding.

Christ has opened our eyes to the truth, so that we know him. So verse 20 concludes, 'We are in him that is true, even in his Son Jesus Christ. This is the true God, and eternal life.' The intimate knowledge of Christ and of being in him that John and other believers experienced was not something they got by their own efforts.

God gave it to them (Matt. 16:17). What do we have that we did not receive from the Father? If we boast of anything, we are untrue to what God has done for us.

So John reminds us that we may continue to grow in assurance by persevering in the knowledge that we have victory over evil, we belong to God, and we have understanding of the true God. Cling to these truths, which the Holy Spirit works and preserves within you. Seek to know them more fully.

## Safeguarding Assurance

John concludes his first epistle with a loving admonition to guard our hearts — a kind of postscript to his letter, which says: 'Little children, keep yourselves from idols' (v. 21). A literal translation of the original Greek is: 'Keep yourselves from *the* idols.' John is thinking of more than the idol worship of first-century pagans (cf. Acts 15:29; 19:23–41; 1 Cor. 8:4,7; 2 Cor. 6:16). He no doubt is referring here to all the false notions of God promoted by the Gnostics and false prophets as well as covetousness — the love of the things that are in the world.

Every age has its temptations. Idolatry abounds today as well as in John's time. Many Christians in Africa and Asia and no doubt elsewhere live side by side with idol-worshippers. Millions of people today call themselves Christians but are still involved in some literal form of idol worship.

In Western culture, we must remember that idolatry does not only mean bowing down to a statue of wood or stone. The heart of idolatry is giving anything or anyone the place that belongs to Christ. Idolatry may be giving what is due to God to a person we love, such as a spouse or a child. It may be giving more attention to a country or a cause than to God, or to an impressive home or a stylish car, a hobby such as gardening or reading, or a blatant lust of the flesh. Often, it is simply focusing too much on ourselves — our own self-righteousness, fame, popularity, or pleasure. It may be giving precedence to our self-imposed ideas about God or our spiritual experiences of him. It may be worshipping our religion or theology instead

of the God of religion and theology. It may be something re-
fined, something gross, or something proposed by evangelical
religion. Whatever it is, if it becomes a controlling matter in our
lives and usurps Christ's place, it is idolatry.

Are we clinging to idols? Do we put other people or things
before Christ? Do we let earthly possessions, such as the com-
puter, our jobs, or even our church work, take priority over our
relationship with Christ?

John knows where the heart of the problem lies. 'Keep
yourselves from idols', he tells us. No one else will do this for us.
We must persevere in guarding our hearts, because idolatry is
an ever present temptation. Such perseverance will enlarge our
assurance, for we know that spiritual watchfulness is the fruit of
the Spirit's saving work.

We keep ourselves from idols by abiding in a right relationship with God, which entails living through the means of grace
in the shadow of Calvary, so that when idolatry offers its attractions, we will be able to see them for what they truly are. Only
the cross helps us guard our hearts, minds, bodies, affections,
and energy, so that we may say with Joseph, 'How then can I
do this great wickedness, and sin against God?' (Gen. 39:9).

Would we keep ourselves from idols? Let us remember the
truth about ourselves, our proneness to fall and our safety in
God. Let us seek grace to walk in fellowship with the Father,
abide in Christ, be filled with the Spirit, and love and do the
truth. Let us centre our lives in the Triune God who loved us,
who sent his Son to save us, who gave his Spirit to indwell us,
and who one day will bring us into his eternal presence.

# 23

## 'For the Truth's Sake'

*The elder unto the elect lady and her children, whom
I love in the truth; and not I only, but also all they
that have known the truth; for the truth's sake, which
dwelleth in us, and shall be with us for ever. Grace be
with you, mercy, and peace, from God the Father, and
from the Lord Jesus Christ, the Son of the Father, in
truth and love.*

*I rejoiced greatly that I found of thy children walking
in truth, as we have received a commandment from the
Father. And now I beseech thee, lady, not as though I
wrote a new commandment unto thee, but that which
we had from the beginning, that we love one another.
And this is love, that we walk after his commandments.
This is the commandment, That, as ye have heard from
the beginning, ye should walk in it.*

*For many deceivers are entered into the world, who
confess not that Jesus Christ is come in the flesh. This
is a deceiver and an antichrist. Look to yourselves, that
we lose not those things which we have wrought, but
that we receive a full reward. Whosoever transgresseth,
and abideth not in the doctrine of Christ, hath not God.
He that abideth in the doctrine of Christ, he hath both
the Father and the Son. If there come any unto you,
and bring not this doctrine, receive him not into your*

*house, neither bid him God speed: For he that biddeth
him God speed is partaker of his evil deeds.*

*Having many things to write unto you, I would not
write with paper and ink: but I trust to come unto you,
and speak face to face, that our joy may be full. The
children of thy elect sister greet thee. Amen* (2 John).

The Apostle John begins his second epistle by designating himself as 'the elder', which can refer to either a church leader or
an elderly person. It probably does not mean that John, in addition to being an apostle, was also an elder in the local church
to which he belonged. Most likely 'the elder' was a title John
acquired through his compelling influence in many churches
over decades.

Second John is addressed to 'the elect lady and her children'. Many people have speculated who this lady and her children were. Some say they were members of a family well known
to John, perhaps even related to him through marriage. Some
say the lady was John's sister-in-law because of the reference in
the last verse to 'sister'.

Others think John was using these terms in a symbolic way,
addressing another local church and its members, since both the
Old and New Testament personify God's church or covenant
community as a woman (Hos. 1-3; Eph. 5:25–33; 2 Cor. 11:2;
1 Peter 5:13; Rev. 19:7–9; 21:2). Today we often speak of the
church as a family or, especially the elect church, as the bride
of Christ. Many speak of the church as 'she' rather than 'it'. So
it would be plausible for John to have spoken of the church in
feminine terms (see vv. 1, 4, 13), as other New Testament writers do (e.g., Eph. 5:21-33).

The lack of distinct personal references throughout this epistle
(in contrast to 3 John) supports the idea that John is addressing
a local church. Moreover, there is a repeated transition from the
second–person singular pronoun (vv. 4, 5, 12) to the second–
personal plural pronoun (vv. 6, 8, 10, 13), which implies that
John was probably thinking of a congregation rather than an
individual.

It is relatively unimportant which of these views is correct because the content of the letter is applicable to both Christian families and the church as Christ's household (Heb. 3:6). The Holy Spirit included this letter in the canon of Scripture because it is relevant to the church and to believers of all times.

The central theme of this little epistle can be summarized in two words that are repeated throughout: *the truth*. Those words refer to the apostolic truth — that is, the teaching committed to John and to his fellow apostles by Christ. John also uses the words *the doctrine of Christ* in verse 9 to refer to apostolic truth. Notice that he says, 'Whosoever transgresseth, and abideth not in the doctrine of Christ, hath not God. He that abideth in the doctrine of Christ, he hath both the Father and the Son.' *The truth* also refers to the Triune God and all the doctrines of the Bible that reveal salvation for sinners in the Father's redeeming grace through Christ and by the Spirit. John tells us that the Father declares the truth (John 1:18), the Son is and brings the truth (John 1:17; 14:6), and the Holy Spirit leads into all truth (John 16:13). This leads believers to know the truth (John 8:32), do the truth (John 3:21), and abide in the truth (John 8:44). All of Christianity is grounded in the truth of the Word of God.

In our day truth is often understood not in terms of right or wrong, but in relative terms. Relativism prevails in the media. People do not think of truth as God thinks of it but rather as something falling between two conflicting positions. But relativism does not fit with the Ten Commandments or any other biblical commandment. If you think like a relativist, you cannot say that it is always wrong to commit adultery or right to live a chaste life. You cannot say that it is always wrong to steal and right to live honestly. You can only say, 'There are circumstances and situations that determine whether something is right or wrong. Adultery — or theft or murder — may be right in one circumstance and wrong in another. It may be wrong today and right tomorrow.'

We live in a culture of situational ethics, but that is not the way biblical writers thought, nor is it the Christian way of thinking. When we turn to the Bible and see what God says about truth, then what is right is true because it is God's truth and he says it. Whatever is contrary to his truth is wrong.

When John and the other apostles speak of the Word of God or the doctrine of Christ as truth, they speak in absolute terms. They speak of something that is true for all people everywhere, for every situation, at all times, because it is *revealed truth*. This truth is not discovered by men, but comes from God through the prophets and apostles who wrote it down for us. God has preserved the truth so that each time we read Scripture, we are confronted with 'the truth', which, for John, ultimately is Christ himself (John 14:6).

John says three things to us in this epistle about truth. Let us examine those one by one.

## A Greeting Grounded in the Truth

The form of John's greeting in verses 1–3 is typical of other greetings in late first-century letters. But the content of the greeting makes it uncommon and distinctly Christian.

The early Christians were definite about the way they greeted one another, in person or in writing. They used such phrases as *Peace be with you* and *Maranatha, the Lord cometh*. Their greetings reflected how they related to each other. Interestingly, similar greetings have appeared from time to time in the history of the church, particularly in times of revival. During the mid-twentieth-century revival in the Scottish Hebrides, for example, it was common for believers to greet one another with the question, 'Have you done business with God today?' During the 1859 revival, Christians often addressed each other by asking, 'Have you heard the good news today?'

John obviously loved to greet believers with a reference to the truth; in the first three verses, he refers to the truth four times. He begins his third epistle similarly, saying, 'The elder unto the well beloved Gaius, whom I love in the truth' (v. 1). John's preoccupation with truth shows his love for it as well as his determination to combat heresy. Many false teachers were infiltrating the church during John's day, causing confusion and spreading lies among believers. John felt burdened to ensure that believers understood the difference between truth and falsehood so that the torch of truth could be handed undimmed to the next generation.

Notice John's love for believers in the truth. He says, 'The elder unto the elect lady and her children, whom I love in the truth; and not I only, but also all they that have known the truth' (2 John 1:1). What a personal greeting! John was writing to people who were in Christ. He deeply loved these believers, and they loved one another in the Lord. The truth was alive in their hearts and lives; it defined them as Christians. It also set them apart from the false teachers who were trying to subvert the church.

Today, in a time many refer to as the ecumenical age, unity is often forced upon professing Christians at the expense of truth. Any unity with others not based on the truth is not Christian unity. If we yield on this point, we will find ourselves on a shifting sea, not knowing where we are or where we are going. Ultimately we will no longer know what truth is.

In verse 2, John professes his love to believers 'for the truth's sake, which dwelleth in us, and shall be with us for ever'. John makes it clear that the love of Christians for each other is rooted in truth. Children of God, we are not told to love one another as Christians because we have similar bank balances, compatible personalities, or similar ambitions. All who have come to know Jesus Christ as the way, the truth, and the life, and who want to spend our lives spreading this truth, should love one another *for the truth's sake*. The truth dwells in us and will be with us forever, John says, so it ought to bind us together in love.

False teachers abandon the truth easily because they are not rooted in the truth. But the true believer perseveres because, by grace, he adheres to the truth of Christ's Word. Jesus said, 'If ye continue in my word, then are ye my disciples indeed; and ye shall know the truth, and the truth shall make you free' (John 8:31-32).

In verse 3, John pronounces a typical divine salutation upon believers: 'Grace be with you, mercy, and peace, from God the Father, and from the Lord Jesus Christ, the Son of the Father, in truth and love.' This salutation contains the content of

a benediction. John stresses 'truth and love' because they are
the context in which these blessings are received.

## A Calling to Walk in the Truth

In verses 4–6, John beseeches his readers to walk in the truth.
He first speaks of the joy he has because the believers to whom
he is writing are walking in the truth: 'I rejoiced greatly that I
found of thy children walking in truth, as we have received a
commandment from the Father' (v. 4a). John rejoices when
his readers adhere to the teachings of the Word of God, obeying them and living according to them. Their walk in the truth
brings joy to his heart — as it does to any true pastor. A pastor
does not find true joy through increasing membership, a new
building, or a higher salary as much as he does when he sees
those to whom he ministers walking in the truth. True joy in a
pastor's heart flows from watching men and women, boys and
girls, being conformed to the image of Christ. True believers are
the real wages of a faithful minister.

Do you bring joy to your church leaders and your parents
because you are walking in the truth?

John describes how to walk in the truth. He says in verses
5 and 6, 'And now I beseech thee, lady, not as though I wrote
a new commandment unto thee, but that which we had from
the beginning, that we love one another. And this is love, that
we walk after his commandments. This is the commandment,
That, as ye have heard from the beginning, ye should walk in
it.' Walking in the truth will express itself in loving one another.
To walk in the truth is to live in accord with the commandments
of God, which are summarized in the word *love*.

John emphasized love in his first epistle (2:7–8), and now
he does it again, saying that he is not introducing a new commandment but an old one that believers have heard from the
beginning. This is something that came from the lips of the
Saviour himself; it is God's own Word, rooted in the Old Testament's admonitions to love one another (Lev. 19:18; Deut.
6:5), and manifested in the highest standard of Christ's own
example (John 13).

Now John tells believers that if they walk in the truth, God's love will surround them and indwell them as a family. In fellowship, they will be given the power to love one another as Christ loved them. When we love one another, we express the nature that Christ has given to us. To love each other truly is to cherish one another as God's image bearers, to seek what is best for each other according to the will of God, and to act toward one another as God commands. That involves listening, helping, praying, giving, and serving each other with kindness and thoughtfulness, forgiving and bearing with one another. It means sharing similar views, similar feelings, similar conflicts, similar interests, similar fears, and similar hopes.

In all these ways we will be distinguished as God's people, for such love defines us as the people of God. As Jesus says, 'By this shall all men know that ye are my disciples, if ye have love one to another' (John 13:35). There is no point in professing to be a disciple of Jesus Christ or professing to walk in the truth of God's Word if we do not love one another. To profess truth and not to love one another is a blatant contradiction. Therefore, 'I beseech thee, lady', John says, for 'this is love, that we walk after his commandments.'

## A Warning Not to Depart from the Truth

In verses 7–11, John issues a warning. He explains why *we need to walk in the truth*: 'For many deceivers are entered into the world, who confess not that Jesus Christ is come in the flesh. This is a deceiver and an antichrist' (v. 7). Notice that the verse opens with the little word *for*. John says that one reason for walking in the truth is that false teachers have gone out into the world. In John's day, those teachers were saying that Jesus Christ did not come in the flesh and that he was not a true man. John says these people oppose the doctrines of Christ, and that the only way to be protected against this false teaching is to know the truth and walk in the truth.

John goes on in verse 8 to explain why *we need to hold onto the truth*: 'Look [take heed] to yourselves, that we lose not those things which we have wrought.' The apostles established churches by preaching the truth of the gospel. Now John is saying, 'If you are going to turn from the truth, then this will collapse!' We need to hold onto the truth so that its bright light will be passed on to the next generation, burning as brightly as when the apostles first received it from the lips of Christ.

We need to stick close to the Word of God. We need to give our lives to the preaching, teaching, and studying of the truth as revealed in Jesus Christ. If we fail to do that, our children — and their children — will be given at best only a dim version of the truth. We will be passing on to them a light that has been so diminished that its clear shining of the truth is no longer visible, and the gospel is no gospel at all. This is already happening in our land today. Many churches offer such a watered-down version of the truth that it no longer has the sound of sovereign grace or the ring of experiential truth. We must warn each other as John did, saying, 'Hold on to the shining light of Scripture. Let God's Word be a lamp to your feet and a light on your path.' As William Bridge wrote, 'Keep the truth and the truth will keep you.'

If we keep the truth, John says, we will 'receive a full reward'. This reward does not refer to meriting salvation but to the gracious reward that flows out of loyal service. Those who value the truth and persistently cling to it will be graciously rewarded with a 'Well done!' from the lips of Jesus. Those who live for themselves and teach false doctrines will lose that reward (see Matt. 7:21–23).

Some believers find it difficult to accept the idea of a reward, knowing what sinners they are. But Jesus spoke often of rewards (see Matt. 5:12; 6:4, 6, 18; 10:41–42; 16:27). Unlike the new birth and salvation, rewards can be lost. When a believer does not persevere in living in truth, as exemplified by love, he loses his reward. False teachers undercut the reward by undoing the work we have done, discouraging us, and damaging our fellowship.

John goes on in verse 9 to explain why *we must continue in the truth*. He says, 'Whosoever transgresseth, and abideth not in the doctrine of Christ, hath not God. He that abideth in the doctrine of Christ, he hath both the Father and the Son.' John makes it clear in his first epistle that continuing in the truth of the gospel is a mark of true faith (1 John 2:18, 19, 22, 23). John states categorically that those who do not continue in the doctrine of Christ do not have God. They do not belong to God, and they are not true Christians. However, those who continue in the doctrine of Christ have the Father and the Son and all his benefits. Continuing in the truth is a crucial mark of true faith.

Finally, John explains why *we must not fellowship with those who corrupt the truth*. He says, 'If there come any unto you, and bring not this doctrine, receive him not into your house, neither bid him God speed: for he that biddeth him God speed is partaker of his evil deeds' (vv. 10–11). Offering Christian fellowship to heretics only confirms them in their heresy. So we are not to welcome false teachers into our spiritual fellowship, John says. We are not to help them spread lies. That does not mean that we are not to speak to such people to reason with them and to correct them, seeking to enlighten them and to bring them to knowledge of the truth. But they are not to be welcomed as true Christians into our homes and churches. We also should not wish them success in their endeavours, their missions, and their deeds because they are engaged in the work of the evil one. They are participating in evil deeds, and if we help them we will be also. That is why we must shun spiritual fellowship with all who seek to corrupt the truth. We are to cling to the truth in the midst of darkness.

Throughout 2 John, the apostle encourages believers to continue walking in love while urging them to be discerning in expressing that love. Truth without love produces severity, but love without truth leads to false sentimentality. Walking in love must never be separated from walking in truth (see Eph. 4:15).

## Closing Lines

John's final words are tender. 'Having many things to write unto you, I would not write with paper and ink: but I trust to come unto you, and speak face to face, that our joy may be full', he writes. 'The children of thy elect sister greet thee' (vv. 12–13). John longs for face-to-face fellowship with believers rather than

communicating with them by letter. But either way, by the Spirit, he wants to fellowship with his brothers and sisters in the faith
as together they enjoy the fellowship of the Father and the Son.
John loves them in the truth.

Do you love the truth and do you fellowship with the saints?
Are you concerned about preserving the truth and about proclaiming it in love? Like John, do you strive to do that 'live and
in person' rather than by letter or e-mail? Do you realize that the
gospel is the only truth that will save sinners, and do you long to
communicate that 'face-to-face'?

If you do not know Jesus as the way, the truth, and the
life, I urge you to flee from the devil's lies. Flee from all teachings that tell you that you only need to be a 'good person' to
get to heaven. Flee from the idea that you only need to attend
church and the Lord's Supper to get to heaven. Be convicted
and transformed by the truth (Rom. 12:1–2). Settle for nothing
less than knowing Jesus Christ as Lord. Then 'ye shall know the
truth, and the truth shall make you free' (John 8:32), and you
will live 'for the truth's sake' (2 John 2).

# 24

# Reactions to the Truth

*The elder unto the well-beloved Gaius, whom I love
in the truth. Beloved, I wish above all things that thou
mayest prosper and be in health, even as thy soul pros-
pereth. For I rejoiced greatly, when the brethren came
and testified of the truth that is in thee, even as thou
walkest in the truth. I have no greater joy than to hear
that my children walk in truth. Beloved, thou doest
faithfully whatsoever thou doest to the brethren, and
to strangers; which have borne witness of thy charity
before the church: whom if thou bring forward on their
journey after a godly sort, thou shalt do well: because
that for his name's sake they went forth, taking nothing
of the Gentiles. We therefore ought to receive such, that
we might be fellowhelpers to the truth.*

*I wrote unto the church: but Diotrephes, who loveth
to have the preeminence among them, receiveth us not.
Wherefore, if I come, I will remember his deeds which
he doeth, prating against us with malicious words: and
not content therewith, neither doth he himself receive
the brethren, and forbiddeth them that would, and
casteth them out of the church. Beloved, follow not that
which is evil, but that which is good. He that doeth good
is of God: but he that doeth evil hath not seen God.
Demetrius hath good report of all men, and of the truth*

*itself: yes, and we also bear record; and yet know that
our record is true.
I had many things to write, but I will not with ink and
pen write unto thee: but I trust I shall shortly see thee,
and we shall speak face to face. Peace be to thee. Our
friends salute thee. Greet the friends by name* (3 John).

Second and Third John are similar in structure, style, and theme.
In both letters John introduces himself as 'the elder'. In both
letters he concludes that he will not write everything because
he hopes to soon see the believers to whom he writes and will
speak with them then. In both letters John offers commenda-
tions for good behaviour and rebukes for bad conduct. And in
both letters his major theme is 'the truth', for in both John is determined to warn believers against false teachers and to protect
from errors that are infiltrating the church of God.

In 3 John, the apostle tells Gaius that he loves him in the
truth (v. 1). In verses 3 and 4, John speaks of walking in the
truth. Verse 8 speaks of 'fellowhelpers to the truth', or allies in
the truth. Then, in verse 12, John speaks of having a good report of the truth. Even in the verses in which the word *truth* is
not specifically mentioned, the focus is still on contending for
the truth.

There is some doubt about whether 2 John is addressed to
an individual or to a church. Third John is obviously a personal
letter, although it concerns the life and welfare of the congregation to which the recipient belongs. The letter is addressed to
Gaius, whom John refers to as 'well-beloved' or a dear friend.

Gaius appears to have been one of John's close Christian
friends who belonged to a church for which John had some
responsibility. John was concerned that this little flock should
learn the truth that Jesus had revealed and made known to
them.

It seems from verses 6 and 7 that John had sent some messengers or teachers to be 'fellowhelpers to the truth' for these
people. Gaius had warmly welcomed these messengers into his
home, but a man named Diotrephes refused to receive those

John had sent and threw them out. John writes that he intended to confront this situation when he visited the church, and, if necessary, exercise discipline. John also writes about a third man named Demetrius, who has a good report of the truth.

Several themes are introduced in 3 John, such as the need to show hospitality to travelling Christian workers, the disastrous consequences of spiritual pride, and the beauty of Christian faithfulness. But 3 John is summarized best through the sketches of the three men John mentions in the epistle. We do not know more about these men than what is mentioned here, but we can learn much from their descriptions in this short epistle.

## Gaius, Loving Upholder of the Truth

The New Testament mentions several men named Gaius. Paul lived in the home of Gaius in Corinth, where he wrote his letter to the Romans (1 Cor. 1:14; Rom. 16:23). A riotous mob at Ephesus seized Gaius of Macedonia along with Aristarchus (Acts 19 and 20). Gaius of Derbe accompanied Paul on his last trip to Jerusalem (Acts 20:4). Every attempt to link John's friend Gaius to one of these Gaiuses has proved futile. That is not surprising, since Gaius, a distinctly Roman name, was one of the most common names in the Roman Empire.

The Gaius John mentions in his epistle faithfully upheld the truth in a local church that John oversaw. John loved Gaius for that, and so he addresses this Gentile Christian in the most cordial and fraternal way: 'The elder unto the well-beloved Gaius, whom I love in the truth' (v. 3). Their love for one another was based on their mutual love of the truth.

Truth is the highest motivation for love. True Christians do not love each other because their temperaments or personalities are compatible, or because they have similar worldly interests or ambitions, but because they love the truths of Christ. When the love of God has renewed their hearts by the Holy Spirit, Christians cannot help loving each other. That is why you find Christians from humble circumstances loving believers who may be higher up the social ladder. In the early Christian church, masters often ate at the same table with the slaves who served them — something unheard of in the Roman Empire. Their love for one another in the truth brought about that kind of mingling. Their mutual love for the Saviour bound them together in the fellowship of the gospel.

Notice that Gaius's commitment to the truth was also evident, and even more significantly so, in how he walked in the truth. John says in verses 3–4: 'For I rejoiced greatly, when the brethren came and testified of the truth that is in thee, even as thou walkest in the truth.'

Gaius 'adorned the doctrine of God' (cf. Tit. 2:10); his entire life showed fidelity to the truth. Just as you would put on a coat to dress yourself, and as the way you dress is evident to all, so our lives should display how we exhibit the truth. We must not only believe and love the truth, but we must also put it into practice in our lives.

Gaius's walking in the truth gave John much joy. The apostle writes, 'I have no greater joy than to hear that my children walk in truth' (v. 4). Some people think Gaius was converted to Christ under John's ministry years before. That may be so. But what really gladdened the heart of John was seeing how Gaius demonstrated in his life clear evidence of being transformed by the truth.

We learn from verses 5 and 8 that Gaius wanted to advance the teaching of the truth; he wanted to help spread the truth. So he was most willing to entertain the Christian mission workers that John sent his way. Gaius was ready to show these workers Christian hospitality, even though they were strangers to him. He was faithful to the truth when he received these brethren, which was what Jesus had told his disciples to do. Jesus said that whenever his disciples went out and were received into homes, 'they received me'. Jesus also said that if anyone gives a cup of cold water to someone, even in the name of a disciple, he will not lose his reward (Matt. 10:42).

Think also of how the writer of Hebrews said, 'Be not forgetful to entertain strangers: for thereby some have entertained angels unawares' (13:2). Gaius was living out the truth in showing hospitality to Christian mission workers. He also sent them on their way in a godly manner, or a manner worthy of God: 'Which have borne witness of thy charity before the church: whom if thou bring forward on their journey after a godly sort, thou shalt do well' (v. 6).

That meant sending workers onward in their journey laden with the necessary provisions, such as necessary food, clothing, and money. John suggests this in verse 7 when he says that these travelling Christian workers went forth to spread the gospel without requesting or receiving any financial support from their pagan neighbours and friends. They went forth in the name of Christ, trusting Christ, and God used faithful men like Gaius to support them. That is a lesson for us in how we are to support the missionary work of the church.

We are not told what position Gaius had in the church. He may have been the minister or an elder in the local church, or he may have been a layperson. Regardless, he worked hard to advance the cause of truth every way he could, including extending hospitality to travelling workers. In this way Gaius became what John describes as a 'fellowhelper to the truth'. He was a fellow labourer, an ally of the truth.

We are taught here that we all have a role in spreading the gospel. Entertaining the messengers of God sent to teach the gospel is a great work; the person who does this is a fellow helper to the truth. If God has reached us with the gospel, and we are assured of the truth in our own hearts, then we are under a moral and spiritual obligation to spread that truth by sharing it with others. Whether at home, on the mission field, or at work, every one of us has a part in proclaiming that message. Every believer, like Gaius, is called to be a faithful upholder of the truth.

Christian hospitality is crucial for the spread of the gospel (Rom. 12:13; Heb. 13:2; 1 Tim. 3:2; 5:10; Tit. 1:8). Hospitality displays Christian faithfulness and love, expresses loyalty to the Lord, and reflects how great God's love is, when it is motivated by love for Christ (3 John 5–8).

In what ways could we encourage this ministry of Christian hospitality? Certainly one way is to be more supportive of our missionaries and of mission work at home and abroad. John tells us how we should treat travelling evangelists and missionaries. We should pray for them, remembering that they are going forth 'for his [Christ's] name's sake' (v. 7). We should give generously to them to relieve them from the temptation to solicit support from unbelievers ('taking nothing of the Gentiles' [v. 7]). We should offer them warm hospitality as fellow workers in the gospel cause ('fellow-helpers to the truth' [v. 8]). We should correspond with missionaries, assuring them of our interest, love, and prayers.

Missionaries treasure 'fellowhelpers'. William Carey, who laboured in India for four decades as a pioneering missionary, used to call his supporters back home in the United Kingdom 'rope holders' because they held the ropes while he was venturing down into what he fondly described as a gold mine in India. We may not be in the front line of battle, but we can share in God's work by supporting those who are. Ask yourself how you could become more like Gaius, so that you might be regarded as one of these 'fellowhelpers to the truth' (v. 8).

John expressed profound love and appreciation to Gaius for exhibiting God's grace. Do we express that kind of love and appreciation to our fellow believers? If not, we should labour to overcome our reluctance to tell them how much they mean to us.

### Diotrephes, Arrogant Opponent of the Truth

In verses 9–11, John tells us about Diotrephes, who belonged to the same church as Gaius but did not appreciate the hospitality being shown to travelling Christians. Diotrephes was arrogant and outspoken in opposing the apostolic authority and message, refusing to welcome those leaders (v. 9). He might have even prevented the church from reading John's letter; hence John wrote this time to Gaius.

John includes himself among the workers rejected by Diotrephes. 'Diotrephes ... receiveth us not' (v. 9). In rejecting these workers, Diotrephes was also opposing the truth of God's Word. The Word of God was divinely communicated to the apostles in the early church before they wrote it down in the books and letters that we now call the New Testament, so Diotrephes was rejecting the testimony that God had given to the truth through John and the apostles. That is why Jesus said when he sent the disciples out, 'He that receiveth you receiveth me, and he that receiveth me receiveth him that sent me' (Matt. 10:40).

The same principle applies today. When people reject the gospel of Christ and the Word that is faithfully preached and taught in the churches, they are not merely turning away from the minister or elders or people in a congregation. If the Word of God is being proclaimed truthfully in that congregation, they are rejecting the authority of our Lord Jesus Christ.

John explains that what motivated Diotrephes's opposition was his love of preeminence. John writes, 'I wrote unto the church; but Diotrephes, who loveth to have the preeminence among them, receiveth us not' (v. 9). We do not know what Diotrephes's position was in the church, whether he was an elected elder or a self-proclaimed leader. Regardless, his problem was not his office but his attitude, motivation, and personality. He was not guided and motivated as a Christian leader ought to be. He was a self-seeker, who wanted to be served, not to serve (Matt. 20:25–28).

The only other time the New Testament uses the word 'preeminence' is in Colossians 1:18, where we read that Christ is the 'head of the body, the church: who is the beginning, the firstborn from the dead; that in all things he might have the preeminence'. Diotrephes's goal was the opposite of what it should have been; he was more concerned for his own glory than he was for the glory of Christ.

A true leader in the church of Christ must be motivated by a deep love and a jealous regard for God's Word. John is warning us here that those who use the church to air their own views and opinions are grasping for a position that God has not given to them. By striving for pre-eminence, they 'lord it over' the church, promoting 'one man rule' in the church, contrary to the entire tenor of the New Testament (cf. Acts 6, 15).

Sadly, Diotrephes lives to some degree inside of each of us. John Newton wrote, 'I have read of many wicked popes, but the worst pope I have ever met is Pope Self.' Diotrephes's problem is our problem by nature. We, too, have a personality problem. Our love for pre-eminence obstructs our love for the truth and for the church.

We need to fight the pride in us that seeks to enthrone ourselves and dethrone God. We must fight it, first, by being aware of its deep roots in us and by knowing how much God hates pride (Prov. 6:16–17). The Bible says that God hates the proud with his heart, curses them with His mouth, and punishes them with his hand (Ps. 119:21; Isa. 2:12; 23:9).

Let us fight pride by asking ourselves, as the Puritan Richard Mayo asked, 'Should that person be proud who has sinned as you have sinned, and lived as you have lived, and has such a heart as you have?'

Most of all, we should fight pride by drawing near to Gethsemane and Calvary's cross. When pride rises in you, consider the contrast between a proud Christian and a humiliated Christ. Confess with Joseph Hall:

*Thy garden is the place,*
*Where pride cannot intrude;*
*For should it dare to enter there,*
*T'would soon be drowned in blood.*

John tells us in verse 10 that Diotrephes expressed his opposition to Christ and the truth in malicious behaviour, 'prating against us with malicious words, and not content therewith, neither doth he himself receive the brethren, and forbiddeth them that would, and casteth them out of the church'. Diotrephes's 'lording it over' the church expressed itself in four ways: First, he spread malicious rumours about the apostle. Second, he rejected those sent to him. Third, he forbad others to receive them. Fourth, he cast out those who received them.

Was Diotrephes a true Christian? John does not tell us directly, though in verse 11, he strongly implies that he was not: John says, 'Beloved, follow not that which is evil, but that which is good. He that doeth good is of God: but he that doeth evil hath not seen God' (v. 11).

Diotrephes certainly was not acting like a Christian. He was attempting to hijack the local church. He needed to be reprimanded. In verse 10 John says that when he came to the church, he would remember Diotrephes's deeds. John planned to initiate disciplinary proceedings against him if he refused to repent of his trouble-making.

Diotrephes was not a heretic. He was not causing trouble in the church like the false teachers in 1 and 2 John. Though his teaching may have been outwardly orthodox, he certainly was not applying the gospel to himself. By rejecting Christ's messengers, he showed that he was an arrogant opponent to the truth.

John concludes this sad section of his letter by telling Gaius not to follow the evil example of Diotrephes. People like him make it clear that they are, at the very least, seriously backslidden. They act like they are not born again and are not of God. Therefore they should be treated as such until they repent.

## Demetrius, Living Testimony for the Truth

Happily, John follows a negative example with a positive one. He talks about Demetrius, who was probably taking John's letter to Gaius and other believers. This man's fidelity to the truth of the gospel was clearly evident to all. As John says, Demetrius 'hath good report of all men' (v. 12a), that is, of all the brothers and sisters in the churches and of those outside the church.

Demetrius was also a living testimony for the truth (v. 12b). He so lived the truth that the truth itself was vindicated through him: 'Yea, and we also bear record; and ye know that our record is true' (v. 12c). Thus, Demetrius is commended by testimonials from John, his fellow Christians, and from his own way of life that flows from living out the truth. What a mentor Demetrius is for us.

John concludes this epistle much as he concludes 2 John, but with a particular reference to Gaius. He writes, 'I had many things to write, but I will not with ink and pen write unto thee: but I trust I shall shortly see thee, and we shall speak face to

face. Peace be to thee. Our friends salute thee. Greet the friends
by name' (vv. 13–14). John's closing words show his warm regard for the believers, urging them to continue exercising love
in the communion of saints. He wants to see his friends 'face to
face', or as it has been translated, 'one by one', fellowshipping
with them and rejoicing over them as they walk in the truth. He
wants fellowship not only with the Father and the Son but also
with the saints, for that is a foretaste of heaven's eternal fellowship.

**Written for Our Example**

Here, then, are three men whom John sets before us. Brief bi-
ographies have been carefully preserved for us in God's Word
as examples for us. In some cases, such as Diotrephes, they are
examples to shun; in other cases, like Gaius and Demetrius,
examples that we should follow.

  Like Gaius and Demetrius, let us recognize that the truth of
the gospel is the only thing that can bring salvation to us and
to those around us. Like these men, let us embrace gospel truth
and direct our lives according to it. Let us place our hope and
confidence for time and eternity in the One who is revealed in
that truth, for he has said, 'I am the way, the truth, and the life:
no man cometh to the Father but by me' (John 14:6).

  Having experienced the life-transforming truth of the gospel
in Christ, let us help spread the good news to others, that we too
may be a good testimony of the truth. Then, with John, we will
view our fellowship in the truth with the Father, the Son, and the
saints as a foretaste of heaven's eternal communion. Our Lord
Jesus Christ will then ever be before us in the perfect church
triumphant, and we will commune with him as the Truth for all
eternity. *Soli Deo gloria!*

# Study Questions

## STUDY 1: Introduction and 1 John 1:1–4

*Introduction*

1. Take twenty minutes to slowly read through 1 John, prefer-
ably aloud, not stopping to ponder phrases but reading for the
overall message. Make your own outline of the book, then list
four of its major themes. How is each of these themes still important today?

2. John wrote this epistle to battle the heresies of Gnosticism
and Docetism. What were these heresies and how can John's
warnings against them be applied today?

3. First John is a book of contrasts (for example, light and darkness) and repetition. List several of these contrasts as well as
several key words and phrases that John repeats often. Why do
you think John uses contrasts and repetition?

*Chapter 1—1:1-2*

4. John presents Jesus as the eternal Son of God, the incarnate
Saviour, the God-man, and the communicator of life. Why is it
important to maintain the views of Jesus that John presents in
these verses? How do these truths show that Christ is the only
one who can meet all our needs? Why is it important to you
that Jesus is the eternal life for needy sinners?

5. In the opening verses of 1 John, the apostle is ravished with Christ. In the busyness of everyday life, how can believers maintain that sense of being ravished with the glorious Saviour?

*Chapter 2—1:3–4*

6. What are four of John's goals in writing this epistle? How are these goals significant today?

7. How does John tie together apostolic doctrine and fellowship with the saints? Why is that link important? How can believers deepen their fellowship with one another?

8. In what ways can we increase communion with the God the Father, God the Son, and God the Holy Spirit?

9. Why do so many believers lack joy? What are some ways of remedying this problem? What role does the Holy Spirit play in helping us experience fulness of joy?

**FOR STUDY 2:** Read 1 John 1:5-10 and chapters 3 and 4.

**STUDY 2: 1 John 1:5–10**

*Chapter 3—1:5–7*

1. What test does John use in verses 5–10 to determine if we are living in fellowship with God? How does God's character serve as a basis for this test (v. 5)?

2. What do *light* and *darkness* symbolize (vv. 5–7; see also John 3:19–21)? List several characteristics of light and darkness.

3. List some texts in Scripture (besides those cited in this chapter) that focus on 'walking with God'. What practical lessons can we learn from these Scriptures?

4. Think about some of your secret sins. Are you asking the Holy Spirit to let the light of God shine upon you so that you will confess and forsake those sins? How can you deal with those sins to regain intimacy with God?

5. What promises are we given if we walk in the light? How will walking in the light enrich our fellowship with other believers? What will help us keep walking in light while we are in the midst of intense affliction?

*Chapter 4—1:8–10*

6. How do we develop wrong attitudes to sin? Since we are not sinless even if we walk in the light, what must we keep doing every day (1:9)?

7. How does our denial or confession of sin belie the reality of our relationship with God? List five advantages of immediately confessing sin to God. How can we make confession of sin more of a habit in our lives?

8. In what ways is the blood of Jesus precious to you?

9. How can God be faithful and just in forgiving our sins? What else does God do when his people confess their sins?

**FOR STUDY 3:** Read 1 John 2:1-6 and chapters 5 and 6.

**STUDY 3: 1 John 2:1–6**

*Chapter 5—2:1–2*

1. What do John's words 'my little children' teach us about what our attitude should be to fellow believers?

2. If Jesus Christ is the complete sacrifice for sinners, what must he think when we try to do something to pay for our sins?

3. How does Christ's propitiatory sacrifice on behalf of believers (v. 2) relate to his advocacy for them (v. 1)? What comfort do true believers find in Jesus' work as their advocate when they do sin?

4. Why is it so important to fight against sin? How can we go on fighting against sin without becoming discouraged by our numerous failures?

*Chapters 6—2:3–6*

5. How would you counsel a friend who claims to be truly sorry for his sins and for hurting others, but says that he can't change because that's the way he is?

6. Define *love*. How can we strengthen a sense of God's love in us?

7. What does John mean by 'the love of God perfected' in us (v. 5)? In what ways are we to 'keep' God's Word?

8. What does it mean to 'walk as Jesus walked'? In what ways can we do what Jesus would do? What helps can we rely on? Should we always do what Jesus would do?

9. What evidences of assurance are there in your life? Can you think of additional evidences that John does not mention here? Based on what John has said, how could you grow in assurance of faith? What hinders your assurance of salvation?

**FOR STUDY 4:** Read 1 John 2:7-14 and chapters 7 and 8.

**STUDY 4: 1 John 2:7–14**

*Chapter 7—2:7–11*

1. Why does John focus on loving our brother as a test of being in the light (vv. 9–11)? What does it mean to 'live in the light'?

2. If you love your brother, you will not cause him to stumble (v. 10). Is this a general principle that normally proves true? When doesn't it hold true? Provide some biblical or personal examples.

3. List some ways in which you could better love others.

4. What area of your life do you need to bring into the light? What obstacles do you face in doing so? How can they be overcome?

*Chapter 8—2:12–14*

5. Explain some ways you are encouraged by what John says to (1) the little children, (2) the young men, and (3) the fathers in grace? How can little children, young men, and fathers grow in grace? What steps can you take to grow in faith?

6. How does the Word of God serve as the source of victory over the evil one? What ways can you use the Word to help you overcome Satan's schemes?

7. What other resources does John say believers have as children of God? How can we use those resources on a daily basis?

**FOR STUDY 5:** Read 1 John 2:15-27 and chapters 9 and 10.

**STUDY 5: 1 John 2:15–27**

*Chapter 9—2:15–17*

1. Define how John uses *world* in this passage. What reason does he give for not loving the world (vv. 15–16)? How can knowing this lessen the world's appeal in your life?

2. What is the second reason we are admonished not to love

the world (v. 17)? How does this tendency play out in politics, fashions, and the world of celebrities? How can knowing this lessen the world's appeal in your life?

3. List some ways in which you can fight against your lustful flesh, lustful eyes, and ungodly pride.

4. Name some activities that have eternal value. How can we help each other value those activities more and worldly activities less?

*Chapter 10—2:18–27*

5. Why is it critical to maintain sound doctrine in the 'last hour' (vv. 18–19)? What is the relationship between perseverance in the faith and our continued work in the church (v. 19)?

6. How does the Holy Spirit help us know the truth and preserve us from error (vv. 20–21, 27)? What danger exists in focusing only on the Holy Spirit when we speak of knowing the truth? How can we counteract that danger?

7. How can there be antichrists before *the* Antichrist comes (v. 22)? What proves that the antichrists were never genuine believers (v. 19)?

8. How would you respond to a Muslim who said to you, 'I don't believe in Jesus, but we believe in the same God' (see v. 23)? Can Muslims or people from other religions who do not believe in Jesus as the Christ be saved?

**FOR STUDY 6:** Read 1 John 2:28 through 3:3 and chapters 11 and 12.

**STUDY 6: 1 John 2:28—3:3**

*Chapter 11—2:28–29*

1. In what ways is abiding in Christ essential for us to meet him confidently when he appears? Describe some ways in which believers can abide in Christ more fully.

2. If you are born again and living close to God, you should also be growing in 'doing righteousness'. Can you say that is true in your life? If so, how could you grow even more in 'doing righteousness'? If you are not 'doing righteousness', what will help you do that?

3. How do you feel about Christ's second coming? What attitude should we have about that?

*Chapter 12—3:1–3*

4. Explain what it means to be adopted by God. What does this say about the greatness of God's love for sinners (vv. 1–2)?

5. Offer some examples comparing the practice of adoption among humans with God's adoption of his children.

6. How does a proper understanding of this doctrine of adoption affect our relationship with God? With the world? With ourselves? With the family of believers? With the future?

7. In verse 2a, what does John say has not yet been fully revealed? What does he tell us that believers do know? How can we live with the tension of knowing yet not knowing in this life?

8. How should we respond to the hope of seeing God's glory and being like Christ (v. 2; see also 1 Cor. 15:42–49; Eph. 4:24; Phi. 3:21)?

9. How does the assurance of Christ's appearing motivate believers to purify themselves (vv. 2–3)? What part do believers have in purifying themselves (v. 3; see also 2 Cor. 7:1; 1 Peter 1:22)?

**FOR STUDY 7:** Read 1 John 3:4-18 and chapters 13 and 14.

**STUDY 7: 1 John 3:4–18**

*Chapter 13—3:4–10*

1. Compare John's definition of sin (v. 4) with current ideas about sin. Why is sin so serious (vv. 4–6, 8–9)?

2. In what ways is sin incompatible with Christ's work on earth (vv. 5, 8)? List two reasons why Christ came into the world, and explain how that should determine our view of sin and our handling of it.

3. Why can't God's people continue to 'live in sin' (vv. 5–9)? What is the difference between living perfectly and living right-eously? How can we, in dependency on the Holy Spirit, per-suade ourselves and others not to sin?

4. How can we determine whether our spiritual parentage is from God or the devil? If you are a child of God, what do you need to change in your life to better reflect that identity (v. 10)?

*Chapter 14—3:11–18*

5. Why is the believer's love for fellow Christians so crucial to his assurance of salvation (vv. 11–15)?

6. Why did Cain murder Abel (v. 12)? Why do wicked people hate righteous people so much? Why shouldn't believers be sur-prised when they are hated by the world (v. 13)? How should we cope with that?

7. In what ways is Calvary God's most profound example of love (v. 16)? According to verses 17–18, in what ways can we follow Christ's example?

8. Why can't true faith remain inactive? Why is it so crucial to pray for, talk with, and witness to people as well as meet their physical and material needs (vv. 17–18)?

9. What are you doing to provide others with what they need? How are you comforting the sorrowful and binding up the broken-hearted? How do you make those who are less fortunate than you feel at home in the church, in your home, and in your community?

**FOR STUDY 8:** Read 1 John 3:19 through 4:6 and chapters 15 and 16.

## STUDY 9: 1 John 3:19—4:6

*Chapter 15—3:19–24*

1. How can John's reassurance in verses 19–20 help us cope with a condemning conscience, spiritual doubt, and spiritual depression?

2. How can we find greater freedom to rest with confidence in God (vv. 21–22)?

3. How do we know that the Holy Spirit is dwelling in us (v. 24)? How can you tell the difference between promptings of the flesh, suggestions of Satan, and the guidance of the Spirit?

4. What would you say to those who struggle with doubts about their faith even though their lives are an open testimony of God's saving grace?

5. Is it possible to exercise faith without love? Is it possible to exercise love without faith? Describe some examples of each.

*Chapter 16—4:1–6*

6. Why must we develop discernment in testing the spirits? List

some ways that we can test the spirits. Is it possible to be too harsh in testing the spirits? Too lenient? Offer some examples of each from Scripture or church history.

7. Why does the antichrist spirit want to destroy the confession that Jesus is God and man? Why is it important to stress both Christ's deity and his humanity in our doctrine of Christ?

8. If Christ were not fully human, what would this mean for our confidence in his revelation of the Father? How would it affect his work on the cross or his return to the Father?

9. How does the antithesis between those who are of the world and those who are of God affect your daily life and relationships? Should it affect you more? In what ways?

**FOR STUDY 9:** Read 1 John 4:17-21 and chapters 17 and 18.

### STUDY 9: 1 John 4:7–21

*Chapter 17—4:7–12*

1. According to John, what is love? Where does it come from? What does it look like? How can it grow? How does God's understanding of love differ from the world's understanding of love?

2. Why is it so important that believers love one another (vv. 8, 11, 12)? How does God's love motivate believers to love those who are difficult to love (v. 11)? How does the love of believers for each other make God's love visible?

3. How can we grow in love without becoming sentimental?

4. Using verses 9–10, explain how believers can show love to believers who have let them down. How can they forgive those who hurt them?

5. In what ways can you show greater love for a brother or sister in Christ this week?

*Chapter 18—4:13–21*

6. Which of John's five sources of assurance do you find most helpful? Why? What other sources of assurance can we draw on in our daily lives that John does not mention?
How will these sources of assurance provide believers confidence on the Judgement Day (vv. 17–18)?

7. What insights does verse 18 provide to explain why we sometimes are afraid of God and others? Explain the relationship between love and fear. How does fear make us unloving?

8. List some of your fears. How can this passage help you surrender those fears to God one by one?

9. If we are believers, what flows out of God's love for us, and why (v. 19)? What flows out of our love for God (v. 21)? What prevents us from loving God?

**FOR STUDY 10:** Read 1 John 4:1-5 and chapters 19 and 20.

## STUDY 10: 1 John 5:1–5

*Chapter 19—5:1–3*

1. What are some inevitable fruits of the new birth (vv. 1–2)?

2. Can love be defined apart from law? Why is obedience to God's commandments possible for those who are born again (v. 3)? Why do even the holiest people often struggle to obey?

3. In what ways do you struggle to obey God? Are there ways to reduce that struggle? What are some of those ways?

*Chapter 20—5:4–5*

4. Define what it means to 'overcome the world'. Who gives us the power to do that? Offer an example from your own life of overcoming the world.

5. Why is it necessary to engage in spiritual warfare in order to overcome the world? In what ways can we rise above this world's way of thinking and resist worldly peer pressure?

6. How does genuine faith in Christ purify the heart?

7. 'Faith looks behind the curtain of sense, and sees sin before it is dressed up for the stage', wrote William Gurnall. What did he mean? How does faith do that?

8. Describe how we can abandon worldliness without falling into legalism.

9. What areas do you need to work on in battling worldliness? According to Scripture, what will help you most in these areas?

**FOR STUDY 11:** Read 1 John 5:6-21 and chapters 21 and 22.

## STUDY 11: 1 John 5:6–21

*Chapter 21—5:6–12*

1. The Old Testament law required two or three witnesses to prove a charge. What are John's three witnesses, and what proof do they offer (vv. 7–8)? Why is it critical that we believe this threefold testimony?

2. Explain why the Christian faith is dependent on historical certainty. What would you say to someone who wanted proof of the gospel?

3. Explain why unbelief is a sin to be deplored, not a misfortune to be pitied. What will happen to those who do not believe in God's testimony of his own Son (vv. 10, 12)?

4. How does your personal experience affirm that eternal life is found only in God's Son (vv. 10–12)? In what ways does the internal witness of the Spirit give you assurance?

5. What trials are you experiencing right now that challenge your faith? How can you increase in faith under these circumstances?

*Chapter 22—5:13–21*

6. How can we be sure that our prayers will be answered (vv. 14–15)? How can prayer help us grow in assurance of salvation?

7. How does the believer experience in sanctification that Christ keeps him and that he keeps himself (v. 18)? How does underemphasizing the former or the latter lead to error?

8. What role does understanding play in our relationship with God?

9. What idols do you need to uproot in your life? How can you guard your heart from idols?

**FOR STUDY 12:** Read 2 John and chapter 23.

**STUDY 12: 2 John**

*Chapter 23—2 John*

1. How many times does John speak of truth in this epistle? What does the emphasis on truth in 2 John say about relativism today?

2. Explain the relationship of truth and love to each other. What are the consequences of having truth without love? Love without truth? What does it mean to love someone 'in the truth' (v. 1)? How can we improve the balance of truth and love in our relationships?

3. We tend to love those who agree with us or are compatible with us. But what does it mean to love them 'for the truth's sake' (v. 2)? How do you suppose your church would change if everyone tried to do this?

4. What gave John great joy (v. 4)? What are some differences between knowing the truth and walking in the truth?

5. What is the difference between John's use of 'commandment' in verse 5 and 'commandments' in verse 6? How is the former important for us? What is the main truth that John emphasizes in verses 5–6? How should this truth affect your life?

6. What do false teachers in John's day and ours refuse to confess (v. 7)? How can we recognize false teachers (v. 9)?

7. What will happen to the reward of people who are led astray by deceivers (v. 8)? How should rewards motivate us in Christian living?

8. To what degree should we fellowship with those who teach false doctrines (vv. 10–11)? Should we shun them? Evangelize them? Befriend them? How can we show love to them?

9. How do John's warnings (vv. 7–11) apply to present-day forms of entertainment? How could you decrease your exposure to ungodly teaching and increase your time with truth? In what ways could you show more discernment in what you watch, read, or hear?

**FOR STUDY 13:** Read 3 John and chapter 24.

**STUDY 13: 3 John**

*Chapter 24—3 John*

1. How is Gaius a good example for us to follow (vv. 2–4)? What does it mean to be 'walking in the truth' (vv. 3–4)? How could we walk in the truth more effectively?

2. In what ways can we show faithfulness to truth and love through Christian hospitality (vv. 5–6)? How does Christian hospitality differ from worldly hospitality? In what ways could we develop greater ministry of Christian hospitality?

3. Verse 6 tells us how we should treat travelling missionaries. In addition to prayer and financial giving, how could you reach out in love to missionaries and support their work?

4. John expressed appreciation to Gaius for his Christian graces. Do you ever express appreciation to fellow believers? If so, give some examples. If not, what hinders you from doing so? How can such hindrances be overcome?

5. How did Diotrephes cause trouble for the church (v. 10)? What did John plan to do about it?

6. Diotrephes lives to some degree inside of each of us. Explain how our natural love for 'pre-eminence' obstructs love for the truth and for fellow believers. In what ways can we fight against pride?

7. Demetrius had a good report of all men (v. 12). What would those who know you best say about your love for the truth and your hospitality? What would your non-Christian neighbours say?

8. Who would be great Christian examples for us to emulate (v. 11–12)? What individuals serve as your mentors for Christian living, and why?

9. How has this study of the epistles of John changed your understanding of the truth and of living the Christian life? With the Spirit's assistance, what changes should you make in your life after studying these epistles?

# Further Reading

*The following books are recommended for the study of John's epistles.*

Barnes, Peter. *Knowing Where We Stand*. Darlington: Evangelical Press, 1998.

Boice, James Montgomery. *The Epistles of John*. Grand Rapids: Zondervan, 1979.

Bruce, F.F. *The Epistles of John*. Grand Rapids: Eerdmans, 1970.

Calvin, John. *Calvin's New Testament Commentaries*. Vol. 5, *The Gospel According to St. John, Part Two, and the First Epistle of John*. Reprint, Grand Rapids: Eerdmans, 1961.

Candlish, Robert S. *The First Epistle of John*. Grand Rapids: Zondervan, 1869.

Cotton, John. *An Exposition of First John*. Evansville, Indiana: Sovereign Grace Publishers, 1962.

Findlay, George G. *Fellowship in the Life Eternal*. New York: Hodder & Stoughton, 1909.

Kistemaker, Simon J. *New Testament Commentary: James and I-III John*. Grand Rapids: Baker, 1986.

Lias, John James. *An Exposition of the First Epistle of John*. London: James Nisbet, 1887.

Morgan, James and Samuel Cox. *The Epistles of John*. Edinburgh: T. & T. Clark, 1865.

Pink, A.W. *Exposition of 1 John*. Grand Rapids: Associated Publishers, n.d.

Stott, John R. W. *The Epistles of John*. London: Tyndale Press, 1964.

## Puritan Reformed Spirituality

In these pages Dr Joel Beeke provides us with a first-class tour of some of the great sites of Reformed theology and spirituality. Here we meet John Calvin, reformer extraordinaire; then we encounter the learned Dr William Ames and the insightful Anthony Burgess. Soon we have travelled north to meet the Scotsmen John Brown of Haddington, the great Thomas Boston and the remarkable brothers, Ebenezer and Ralph Erskine.

Predictably, but happily our guide brigs us to The Netherlands and to the time of the Nadere Reformatie, before taking us back to the New World in the company of the remarkable Theodorus Jacobus Freylinghuysen.

But the climax of this tour is not reached until our trusted guide has brought us to the family roots from which all these theologians and pastors came — to the strong foundations of Christian living in justification by faith and sanctification in life, nourished by the power of biblical preaching.

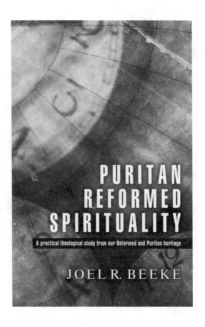

Spirituality is a subject much on the minds of people today. With its prevailing secularism and materialism, modern culture has failed to satisfy its consumers. The result is a new interest in discovering and nurturing the inward, spiritual dimensions of human life. This book promotes biblical spirituality through a study of the Reformed and Puritan heritage.

ISBN: 0 85234 629 8

*A wide range of Christian books is available from Evangeli-cal Press. If you would like a free catalogue please write to us or contact us by e-mail. Alternatively, you can view the whole catalogue online at our website:*

www.evangelicalpress.org.

**Evangelical Press**
Faverdale North, Darlington, Co. Durham, DL3 0PH, England
e-mail: sales@evangelicalpress.org

**Evangelical Press USA**
P. O. Box 825, Webster, New York 14580, USA
e-mail: usa.sales@evangelicalpress.org